The Washington Papers/166

NAFTA
What Comes Next?

Sidney Weintraub

Foreword by
Paul A. Volcker

PUBLISHED WITH
THE CENTER FOR STRATEGIC
AND INTERNATIONAL STUDIES
WASHINGTON, D.C.

Westport, Connecticut
London

Library of Congress Cataloging-in-Publication Data

Weintraub, Sidney, 1929–
    NAFTA : what comes next? / Sidney Weintraub.
      p. cm. – (The Washington papers ; 166)
    "Published with the Center for Strategic and International Studies
Washington, D.C."
    Includes index.
    ISBN 0-275-95118-9 (cloth : alk. paper). – ISBN 0-275-95119-7
(pbk. : alk. paper)
    1. Free trade – North America.   2. North America – Economic
integration.   3. Canada Treaties, etc. 1992 Oct. 7.   I. Title.
II. Series.
HF1746.W44   1994
382′.917 – dc20   94-23323

The *Washington Papers* are written under the auspices of the Center for
Strategic and International Studies (CSIS) and published with CSIS by
Praeger Publishers. CSIS, as a public policy research institution, does not
take specific policy positions. Accordingly, all views, positions, and
conclusions expressed in the volumes of this series should be understood
to be solely those of the authors.

British Library Cataloging in Publication data is available.

Library of Congress Catalog Card Number: 94-23323
ISBN: 0-275-95118-9 (cloth)
       0-275-95119-7 (paper)

First published in 1994

Praeger Publishers, 88 Post Road West, Westport, CT 06881
An imprint of Greenwood Publishing Group, Inc.

Printed in the United States of America

The paper used in this book complies with the Permanent
Paper Standard issued by the National Information Standards
Organization (Z39.48-1984).

10 9 8 7 6 5 4 3 2

NAFTA
What Comes Next?

THE WASHINGTON PAPERS

... intended to meet the need for an authoritative, yet prompt, public appraisal of the major developments in world affairs.

MANUSCRIPT SUBMISSION

The Washington Papers and Praeger Publishers welcome inquiries concerning manuscript submissions. Please include with your inquiry a curriculum vitae, synopsis, table of contents, and estimated manuscript length. Manuscript length must fall between 120 and 200 double-spaced typed pages. All submissions will be peer reviewed. Submissions to *The Washington Papers* should be sent to *The Washington Papers*; The Center for Strategic and International Studies; 1800 K Street NW; Suite 400; Washington, DC 20006. Book proposals should be sent to Praeger Publishers; 90 Post Road West; P.O. Box 5007; Westport, CT 06881-5007.

To Gladys—
who I suspect believes that
my infatuation with NAFTA
has gone on far too long

Contents

List of Tables

Foreword

Regionalism has emerged as one of the defining forces of the world economy in the latter part of the twentieth century. Although the specific efforts vary in scope and intent, the general trend is unmistakable. The European Union – the old Common Market – is both the earliest and strongest manifestation, with an ambitious agenda to develop a shared political and economic identity. At the other end of the spectrum are looser and smaller associations. The ASEAN group in the Asia-Pacific area and MERCOSUR and other limited arrangements in Latin America are examples. The regional arrangements in North America lie somewhere between. The North American Free Trade Agreement (NAFTA) lacks the historic motivation of the European Union to pool national sovereignty. Yet it does reflect an intensively negotiated framework to codify free trade and investment and reaches into other areas of economic life, breaking ground on environmental and other issues.

The rise of regionalism poses many important questions about the future of the international economy. How will the process of regional deepening evolve? Where will regional perimeters be set? Will national governments be willing to accept the implied loss in national autonomy with respect to economic (and increasingly other) decisions that comprehensive agreements imply? Will, in the end, regional accords promote an open world economy or undermine it?

This new assessment of NAFTA and its potential casts fresh light on these questions, and no one is better placed to analyze the issues than Sidney Weintraub. I first came to know Dr. Weintraub when our governmental responsibilities, from different organizational perspectives, brought us into frequent contact. I was at the time Treasury's "international" man; he was the State Department's "economist." In that role, he did a great deal to bring greater recognition of the economic dimension of international relations into U.S. foreign policy formulation. I suspect he took satisfaction in educating me about the foreign policy implications of economic policy.

This work reflects Dr. Weintraub's capacity for conceptual thinking, his economist's understanding of the issues, and his long experience, within government and as a scholar, with Latin American affairs.

Dr. Weintraub makes three points of particular interest to policymakers and researchers. First, he draws a useful distinction between "strong" and "weak" regional integration. Comprehensive regional economic arrangements, such as those envisioned in NAFTA, are not only more difficult to achieve but potentially more beneficial than more limited trade and investment measures. In his view, the successful deepening of the North American economic integration remains the surest way to keep NAFTA compatible with an open world economy. It also provides the most durable foundation for widening NAFTA's membership. Rather than enlargement, however, given protectionist pressures in Canada, Mexico, and the United States, Dr. Weintraub urges that the painstaking task of making NAFTA itself work be regarded as a priority challenge.

Second, Dr. Weintraub highlights the trend toward subregional integrations in the Western hemisphere. The growing recognition that free trade arrangements can serve as an engine of growth rather than a protective barrier marks a fundamental change in Latin perspectives. The United States has a significant stake in the efforts that are under way to deepen economic relationships within the Southern Cone, the Andes, Central America, and the Caribbean. Indeed, subregional integration may provide the most effective long-term building block to expand NAFTA.

Third, the author warns against the helter-skelter widening of the North American Free Trade Agreement. Although the United States has every reason to support hemispheric economic integration, the path to that objective will shape the eventual outcome. A series of ad hoc bilateral free trade negotiations within the hemisphere, for example, could undercut prospects for wider regional cooperation.

I am among those who have approached the current fashion toward regionalism with a certain amount of skepticism, concerned about the ultimate impact on the broader multilateral system and the General Agreement on Tariffs and Trade (GATT). So far, my concern that regional "free trade" arrangements may turn out to be a rationalization for regional insularity has not been borne out. But the danger remains unless we in fact persist in our effort to build stronger and broader understandings and arrangements internationally.

However useful and justified NAFTA is in the particular circumstances of North America in the 1990s – and I strongly believe it is – I doubt that it is a logical model for extension to other regions. Indeed, when one looks to the dynamic Pacific Rim, which will properly play a larger role within U.S. global interests, the Asia-Pacific Economic Cooperation (APEC) framework, at once both looser and broader, provides a more suitable basis for policy initiative. And, as I write, I am aware that the U.S. Congress has not yet approved GATT, agreed to many months ago after years of difficult negotiation.

As Dr. Weintraub would be the first to point out, NAFTA can be only one component of an intelligent U.S. response to the shifting scene of global economies.

Paul A. Volcker

About the Author

Sidney Weintraub holds the William E. Simon Chair in Political Economy at the Center for Strategic and International Studies and is also Dean Rusk Professor of International Affairs at the Lyndon B. Johnson School of Public Affairs, the University of Texas at Austin. Before joining the LBJ School, Dr. Weintraub was a career foreign service officer of the U.S. Department of State working primarily on issues of international trade, finance, and development. He has written extensively on North American economic integration, including a book published by the Brookings Institution in 1984 with the prophetic title *Free Trade between Mexico and the United States?* His volume *A Marriage of Convenience: Relations between Mexico and the United States*, published by Oxford University Press in 1990, has just come out in a Spanish edition published by Editorial Diana in Mexico City under the title *Matrimonio por Conveniencia*.

Acknowledgments

I have lived in Austin, Texas, since 1976, and proximity has given me much opportunity to visit Mexico frequently. When I moved to Washington, D.C., in mid-1993, the U.S. debate on whether to approve NAFTA was in full swing. My presence in Washington permitted me to observe this debate first hand, particularly in the U.S. Congress, and to interact directly with key players. I thank CSIS, particularly the chairman of its Board of Trustees, Anne Armstrong, and its president, David Abshire, for giving me this opportunity.

Many people have contributed to my thinking about NAFTA and what must happen now that it is in place. I will not attempt to name them here. A process of learning by osmosis takes place in Washington. There are what seems to be an infinite number of meetings of specialists on every conceivable aspect of an issue as hotly contested as NAFTA. Individuals and institutions, both those for and against the agreement, came to Washington to influence the outcome. Participating in and listening to congressional hearings is a valuable learning experience. CSIS and the Carter Center at Emory University in Atlanta joined together to create a NAFTA and Beyond Commission, to which I contributed. I owe special thanks to M. Delal Baer, who directs the Mexico project at CSIS and who was the executive director of the commission. Similarly, I give special thanks to Georges Fauriol, who directs the Americas Program at CSIS. I discussed all aspects of NAFTA and beyond with both Delal and Georges, and their insights influenced my thinking. Gary C. Hufbauer and Brad Roberts kindly reviewed the manuscript and provided valuable suggestions.

Nancy Eddy, who directs the publications program at CSIS, gently reminded me from time to time that I had promised to write this monograph. Donna Spitler, also from the publications program, asked me if I planned to write the manuscript, and her reminders served as a prod to get down to business. Donna edited this manuscript with skill and speed, and I thank her for that. This manuscript would never have seen the light of day without the tireless and amiable assistance of Carolyn Blackwell, my assistant at CSIS.

Abbreviations

AD	Antidumping duty
AFL–CIO	American Federation of Labor–Congress of Industrial Organizations
ALADI	Latin American Integration Association (from the Spanish initials)
ANCOM	Andean Common Market
CACM	Central American Common Market
CARICOM	Caribbean Community and Common Market
CBI	Caribbean Basin Initiative
CET	Common External Tariff
CGE	Computable General Equilibrium Model
CIEPLAN	Corporación de Investigaciones Económicas para Latinoamerica (a Chilean research group)
CUFTA	Canada-U.S. Free Trade Agreement
CVD	Countervailing duty
EAI	Enterprise for the Americas Initiative
EC	European Community
EC-92	The EC program to achieve a unified market by 1992
ECLA	UN Economic Commission for Latin America

ECLAC	UN Economic Commission for Latin America and the Caribbean
EEC	European Economic Community
EFTA	European Free Trade Association
EMU	Economic and Monetary Union (in the European Union)
EU	European Union
FDI	Foreign Direct Investment
FTA	Free Trade Area
GATT	General Agreement on Tariffs and Trade
GDP	Gross Domestic Product
G-3	Colombia, Mexico, and Venezuela in their efforts to reach free trade among the three countries
IDB	Inter-American Development Bank
INS	U.S. Immigration and Naturalization Service
LAC	Latin America and the Caribbean
MERCOSUR	Southern Cone customs union program among Argentina, Brazil, Paraguay, and Uruguay
MFN	Most Favored Nation
MNC	Multinational Corporation
MOFA	Majority-Owned Foreign Affiliate
NADBank	North American Development Bank
NAFTA	North American Free Trade Agreement
NGO	Nongovernmental Organization
OAS	Organization of American States
OECS	Organization of Eastern Caribbean States
PRI	Institutional Revolutionary Party of Mexico
SELA	Latin American Economic System
TRIMs	Trade-Related Investment Measures
UK	United Kingdom
UN	United Nations
U.S.	United States
USITC	U.S. International Trade Commission
WHFTA	Western Hemisphere Free Trade Area

Summary

After a bitter debate in the United States, the North American Free Trade Agreement (NAFTA) came into effect among Canada, Mexico, and the United States on January 1, 1994. The agreement provides a detailed framework for the conduct of trade among the three countries. But its objectives are much more expansive than trade alone: The agreement is designed to remove barriers to investment among the three countries, permit the free flow of services, and enable expeditious settlement of trade disputes. NAFTA is an economic agreement that should influence where and how goods are produced and how services are provided in North America; the words "free trade" in its title are a form of shorthand for a much broader understanding.

If NAFTA works as its supporters posited, it should have a positive effect on income and employment in each of the three member countries. These effects should be greatest in Mexico, the least developed of the three. If there are not mutual benefits, then the agreement is unlikely to endure. The gains, however, depend on adding content to the framework provided by the agreement. This deepening must necessarily involve, among other things, more efficient customs procedures, understandings on common or compatible standards for industrial goods, working out sanitary requirements for food and pharmaceutical products, enhanced environmental protection, and consistent standards for trucks that in due course will have the right to carry freight anywhere in North America.

Deepening deals primarily with relations among the three NAFTA countries. NAFTA, if it works as contemplated, inevitably will also be a magnet for other countries. The potential widening of NAFTA was given much stimulus by the U.S. proposal for Western Hemisphere free trade from Alaska in the north to Tierra del Fuego off the southern tip of Chile. Chile, in fact, already has indicated its desire to accede to NAFTA.

But there are profound differences between widening to the southern tip of the hemisphere and economic integration within a contiguous region. Production, transportation, environmental, and customs problems are vastly different between the United States and its two land neighbors from what they are between North and South America. There can thus be tension between the two phenomena that are in play—the deepening of NAFTA within the North American region and the widening of the agreement to new and more geographically distant countries. This volume lays out guidelines for dealing with this potential tension, for how to facilitate deepening while still contemplating widening.

One other major theme must be considered. Latin American and Caribbean countries during the last decade have made a radical change in development philosophy. From what earlier had been a policy of promoting domestic industry behind high import barriers, the region shifted to more open markets. This was largely done unilaterally— that is, without seeking reciprocity. The motive was to encourage exports, particularly of manufactured goods with a high valued-added content. The philosophic change was prompted by severe economic problems during what the Latin Americans refer to as the lost decade of the 1980s.

Regional integration arrangements have been reinvigorated throughout the hemisphere. Earlier integration agreements were designed to widen subregional markets behind high barriers; the new version is intended to encourage efficiency under what is known as "open integration." These subregional economic integration agreements now exist in the Southern Cone of South America, among the Andean countries, in Central America, and in the Caribbean. In addition to the potential incompatibilities between the deepening and widening of NAFTA, there is considerable tension as to which should take priority—the deepening of subregional agreements throughout the hemisphere or the goal of hemispheric free trade through rapid accession of countries to NAFTA.

This volume argues that priority should be given to subregional integration because the economic payoff is greatest if this policy is followed. Subregional agreements are the best stepping stones to hemispheric economic integration.

There is greater mutuality of interest between the United States and the rest of the hemisphere than has existed at any time in the recent past. Most Latin American and Caribbean countries are now democracies. Their development philosophy—placing greater stress than before on the workings of the market and opening their own markets to import competition—dovetails well with that of the United States. North America as well as other hemispheric subregions are seeking greater economic integration behind low barriers against outsiders. Under their new philosophy, what other countries of the hemisphere most want is assurance of access to the markets of each other and the United States for their competitive goods and services.

This common thinking is what makes the present a most propitious moment for hemispheric cooperation. This volume was written in the hope that the current opportunity for cooperation is not frittered away.

NAFTA
What Comes Next?

1

Introduction

The text of the North American Free Trade Agreement (NAFTA), as voluminous as it is, essentially provides a framework to which content must be added. Many decisions are required now that the agreement is in force. The choices made can lead to a superficial, and hence unstable, enterprise or ensure that NAFTA will develop into a significant endeavor deepening the relationships among the three member countries. NAFTA can remain a closed "club of three" – Canada, Mexico, and the United States – or it can grow into a hemispheric enterprise and potentially extra-hemispheric as well. It can develop into an example of "strong" integration that goes beyond simple trade and investment preferences, or it can be simply a "weak" integration that is only skin deep. This volume examines the various choices and their implications.

NAFTA, when viewed as a framework, can be compared to a constitution. The U.S. Constitution, as magnificent as the original document was, provided no guarantee about how the separation of powers among the three branches would develop, or what the substance of the first amendment would turn out to be, or even that there would be a common market among the initial and subsequent states. Each of these developments resulted from an accumulation of decisions, mostly building on what went before. The constitution of the former Soviet Union was also a remarkable document, but it turned out to be a facade for repression and not a guide to action. Mexico, despite its formal name of the United States of Mexico, developed a highly centralized form of federalism quite different from that between the federal government and the separate states of the United States of America. Canada's confederation to this date has not been transformed into a common market in which barriers to trade among the provinces have been eliminated. Trade may be freer between Canada and the United States than between the provinces of Canada.

NAFTA was approved only after considerable debate, much of it highly contentious. No recent trade agreement entered into by the United States was as divisive as NAFTA. This was not because NAFTA was more important in trade terms than other negotiations, such as the Uruguay Round of the General Agreement on Tariffs and Trade (GATT), which was concluded in December 1993, the month after the enabling legislation for NAFTA was approved. GATT has 124 members. U.S. worldwide exports were $465 billion in 1993; U.S. exports to the other two NAFTA countries in 1993 were $142 billion.

Yet NAFTA differs from other trade agreements. For one reason, despite the words "free trade" in its name, it is much more than a trade agreement. NAFTA is intended to encompass an array of economic relations beyond trade in goods and services, such as investment, transportation, communications, border relations, environmental and labor matters, just to name a few. Stated more provocatively, NAFTA has the potential to alter political relations among the three countries in ways not possible in a global organization.

A second reason is that NAFTA represents attention to neighborhood, especially as it encompasses Mexico, a country much poorer and less open politically than the other two, and one with a cultural tradition sharply different from those of Canada or the United States. Indeed, it was these economic, political, social, and cultural differences around which the NAFTA debate revolved in the United States and in the other two countries as well.

The next stage – implementing the agreement – is already taking place, but with relatively little publicity. Representatives of the three governments, and from the three private sectors and nongovernmental organizations (NGOs), are negotiating across national lines in a variety of fields and will thereby affect how goods are produced, how financial institutions operate, what sanitary requirements apply to imports, and how to determine the safety and emissions standards for trucks and motor vehicles that cross national boundaries. The individual measures will be incremental, each building on earlier decisions, and few individual actions will be spectacular or controversial enough to attract widespread attention. The media will not focus on these seemingly technical issues the way they did on the conflicts that generated the NAFTA debate.

This volume serves as a guide to the kinds of decisions that must be made in the years ahead and what their implications might be. It does not substitute for media attention, but instead provides context when a particular subject surrounding the operations of NAFTA does attract national attention.

The Choices

Two types of decisions will have to be made. The first area, which is quite broad, determines whether member countries wish to deepen and institutionalize their relations under NAFTA or, alternatively, to maintain a classic preferential area in which member countries – the three current members and any others later admitted – simply enjoy trade, investment, and related production advantages over nonmember countries. These can be called macro decisions.

There are conflicting clues in the basic agreement about the intention of the framers. The dispute-settlement provisions of chapter 19, dealing with antidumping (AD) and countervailing duty (CVD) matters, are an example of a broad view of NAFTA, one intended to institutionalize dispute settlement across North America rather than isolate this in the individual countries. Chapter 19 draws heavily on a similar chapter in the Canada-U.S. Free Trade Agreement (CUFTA). But, even this "North American" chapter was necessitated by U.S. insistence on treating AD and CVD matters as a national prerogative rather than accepting the logic of free trade; there are no internal AD or CVD provisions for trade among the states of the United States as there are for North American trade. The rules of origin for textile, apparel, and automotive trade take a narrow view, one that looks primarily toward a constrained preferential area.

The second area of necessary decisions involves the operating details of carrying out the agreement. Working parties and committees are already at work to make recommendations on issues such as possible acceleration of the tariff reductions set forth in the agreement; techniques to facilitate the movement of goods across borders, including improved customs clearance; whether there is a need to revise the rules of origin, especially for trade in apparel and textiles and automotive products; and to hammer out sanitary and phytosanitary safeguards for trade in agricultural products. This is but a small sample of what can be called the micro decisions that will be required.[1] There is a gray area in which the macro and micro areas merge — issues dealing with competition policy, for example.

The macro decisions are matters of "high" policy, to use a term familiar to analysis of international relations. They set the overall schema within which the day-to-day micro decisions will be made. This combination of macro institutionalization and micro implementation is reflected in the issue of regulatory actions. Governments constantly issue new regulations. More than 65,000 pages of proposed regulations were published in the U.S. *Federal Register* in 1993.[2] NAFTA will stimulate much new regulatory action in such fields as product, environmental, sanitary, and labor standards. New regulations will be issued by national governments and by governments at other levels as well. Regulations can be constructed to facilitate trade or to impede it. Environmental regulations can increase or diminish the level of environmental protection; they can be subterfuges for trade protection as well. A regulation can be written with the domestic situation in mind, but then sideswipe the economy of other member countries out of sheer ignorance or disregard of other national practices.

The best way to deal with this complexity is to work out procedures under which each member country is able to penetrate the regulatory processes of the others. This is not a simple task in view of the sheer volume of regulatory activity. It is not just governments that must be able to enter into the regulatory processes of other governments, but also private parties (for example, in the setting of product standards) and NGOs on issues such as the environment, labor, and trucking standards. Professional groups within countries – doctors, accountants, lawyers, and even producers of goods when they set standards for an industry – issue regulations on their own authority that can affect trade in goods and services. The macro issue that must be dealt with in the regulatory field is how to combine transparency and timeliness in permitting non-national access to regulatory procedures. Once the macro structure is established, then this framework can kick into high gear at the micro level.

Absent this ability of cross-border penetration, the economic integration in North America is unlikely to deepen profoundly because of the importance of regulatory activity in determining the production and delivery of goods and services. The decision on how to deal with national regulations will be a crucial determinant of whether NAFTA evolves into an example of "strong" or "weak" integration.

There are other areas in which the question of institutionalizing a NAFTA process must be decided. These include the setting of standards for industrial products to facilitate production of components anywhere in the region for later assembly somewhere else; the structure for advance consultation on major policy issues, such as each country's macroeconomic plans, to permit input by the others and to give them time to take these plans into account in their own policies; and the manner of cooperation between central banks on exchange-rate issues.

Deepening of NAFTA into a strong form of integration will also require dealing with issues that ostensibly are extraneous to the economic integration agenda but that inevitably impinge on the process. These include cooperation on migration and drug traffic, and the speed with which Mexico opens its political process. My strong conviction is that the deepening and institutionalization necessary for strong integration require some assurance in both the United States and Canada that Mexico is able to transform itself from an authoritarian to a more open, democratic society.[3]

Deepening versus Widening

There was considerable debate in the European Community (EC) for many years between the deepeners and the wideners. The deepeners wanted Community authority over many aspects of economic policy that the wideners preferred to maintain as national prerogatives. Put in what may be overly simple form, the wideners hoped that by expanding EC membership, the political and economic integration in Europe would not become too intrusive. Wideners, like Margaret Thatcher and even to a great extent John Major, have preferred more freedom for national governments in making social policy; they would like to abandon the goal of monetary union, at least in the foreseeable future. The transformation of the EC into the European Union (EU) was, on the surface, a victory for the deepeners—"on the surface" because a common EU currency and the single central bank envisaged in the Maastricht decisions may not come into existence soon.

The term "deepening," which comes from EC debates, may have too much regional baggage to describe the process that must take place in NAFTA, which does not contemplate a single currency or a supranational institution that has the power to formulate directives that eventually become national law. Even the most naive observer knows that the situations in Western Europe and North America are dissimilar. The theoretical end objective of the EU — political union — is absent in North America or the Western Hemisphere generally. A free trade area was chosen as the integration technique in North America because this permits each member country to have its own external tariff and commercial policy. A free trade area has less political content than a customs union, which calls for a common external tariff and common commercial policy. There is less derogation of sovereignty in a free trade area than there would be in a common market, which implies freedom of migration from one country to another.

Yet, NAFTA will have its own institutional development, and the more it widens to additional countries, the more elaborate its institutions will have to be. To cooperate on regulatory procedures, in settling disputes, in working out environmental, labor, transportation, communication, and product standards, and in ensuring the ability of nationals of member countries to provide financial and other services across borders requires institutionalizing many economic issues on a North American level. The more rapidly NAFTA widens to admit other members, whether in the Western Hemisphere, Asia, or elsewhere, the more difficult it will be to work out the deepening among the three countries in North America. The more rapidly NAFTA is widened, the more likely it is that the integration will be weak — a preferential arrangement rather than a truly integrative one.

The difference between the two outcomes is not trivial.

Today's main trade impediments in North America are not tariffs, but rather restrictions on investment, inadequate protection of intellectual property, stifling of competition both within and across countries, regulations deliberately designed to protect domestic industry and national service providers, and the use of contingent protection, like ADs and CVDs. Laborious customs procedures can be more costly than modest tariffs. Exchange-rate manipulation can have a far greater impact on trade than tariffs; the magnitude of the swings in the U.S. and Canadian dollar relationship after CUFTA went into existence were many times larger than the tariffs that were being reduced.[4] The differences in the way social services, such as health care, are provided can have an impact on relative production costs substantially more significant than a modest border tariff. The business communities of the three NAFTA members will force the authorities to take account of these issues regardless of the initial intent of the three governments.

It is worth noting that four countries of the European Free Trade Association (EFTA) – Sweden, Finland, Austria, Norway – have negotiated to join the EU despite the fact that EFTA and the EU have a free trade agreement. Eliminating tariffs is evidently not enough. The EFTA countries also wish to have a voice in making decisions on the related issues that transcend the border barriers.

The EC – now the EU – handled this inherent conflict between deepening and widening by deepening first among the existing members, then admitting some new members who accepted the newly deepened arrangement, then deepened further and widened further. Great differences exist between Western Europe and the Western Hemisphere, and their objectives for eventual economic union also differ. Yet the European procedure on handling issues of strengthening internal discipline, before widening to new members who would have to accept this new discipline, may serve as a model for NAFTA.

The way that widening is handled will also influence the structure of North American and Western Hemisphere integration. The Western Hemisphere is replete with subregional economic integration arrangements. There are also cross-memberships in which individual countries are members of various groupings. Venezuela and Colombia, for example, are members of the Latin American Integration Association (ALADI, from its name in Spanish) and the Andean group, and are joined with Mexico in a free trade agreement (the G-3 as it is known). Mexico, in addition to being a member of NAFTA, has free trade agreements with Chile and Costa Rica, plus the G-3, and is negotiating for free trade with Central America.

If the major subregional economic groupings in Latin America and the Caribbean wish to deepen their own arrangements, it would be desirable for them to affiliate with NAFTA as subregions. For example, the MERCOSUR group (Brazil, Argentina, Uruguay, and Paraguay) could negotiate as a single unit with the single unit of NAFTA. Yet, it is not clear that is what Argentina wishes; its authorities have indicated a desire to accede to NAFTA. Chile, other than its free trade arrangement with Mexico and others, is not a member of any subregional group and has made clear that it wishes to accede to NAFTA. But the issue is more complex when individual members of Latin American and Caribbean subregional groups are prepared to discard the subregional arrangement and adhere to NAFTA, or when Costa Rica chooses both membership in a Central American grouping and free trade with Mexico. The way these situations are handled will influence both the structure of NAFTA and the development of trading arrangements in the hemisphere.

It is not clear either whether the U.S. government prefers widening via accession to NAFTA over negotiating a separate U.S. bilateral agreement with each country. If the latter path is followed, the United States could then be a member of NAFTA and have bilateral free trade areas with, say, Chile, then perhaps Argentina.

Under these circumstances, the Canadians might then find themselves forced to sign a separate free trade agreement with these countries to avoid a situation in which their free trade arrangements are narrower than those of the United States. If Canada had free trade only with Mexico and the United States, but the United States separately had free trade with many more countries, this would make Canada less attractive as a location for foreign investment.

Joining NAFTA was Canada's way to avoid a hub-and-spoke arrangement under which only the United States had free trade with many countries and Canada was but one spoke to the U.S. hub. The issue of hub-and-spoke is far from dead in U.S. thinking. The spokes may not be just in this hemisphere, but may extend to Asia as well. There is much speculation in the United States that trade arrangements only with countries in this hemisphere are inadequate because they omit the world's fastest growing economies.

Sovereignty

The required macro decisions, therefore, deal with the extent of deepening within the North American region itself, how this is institutionalized, and then how this deepening may be affected by widening the area of free trade in this hemisphere and elsewhere. As each of these decisions is made, the institutional structure for these arrangements will have to be altered.

The United States, to put it succinctly, must decide what its main objective is. Is it to construct a strong integration arrangement in North America and then use that as the base from which to widen to other countries? Or is it to seek a weak form of integration as broadly based geographically as possible in order to exploit trade preferences over a large portion of world trade?

The issue of deepening has sovereignty implications. Although they are not as extensive as those in the EU because the end objective in the Western Hemisphere is less ambitious than in Europe, they exist nevertheless. The penetration by each NAFTA member into the regulatory processes of the others involves some derogation of national sovereignty in favor of a broader definition. The dispute-settlement arrangement under chapter 19 of NAFTA under which binational panels can make binding arbitration decisions on how countries are carrying out their own AD and CVD laws and regulations is a way of bypassing national courts. The two supplemental agreements on the environment and labor still leave most decisions on these issues in national hands, but they do contemplate outside monitoring of each country's performance.

When NAFTA was negotiated, Mexico first resisted including material on labor standards and the environment. At U.S. insistence, these issues were included in the body of the NAFTA text. Then presidential candidate Bill Clinton asserted that these provisions were inadequate and supplemental agreements were required. Mexico resisted, but then assented and indeed made concessions on potential trade penalties for consistent violation of its own standards. These are not major derogations of Mexican sovereignty in that the potential penalties are insulated by complex procedures, but they are intrusions. They were extracted under the pressure exerted by interested parties in the United States as the price of obtaining congressional approval of NAFTA.

Many members of the U.S. Congress opposed NAFTA on the ground that Mexico had an authoritarian regime and the United States should not enter into a free trade agreement with a country in which there are many charges of violation of human rights and whose electoral process is flawed. There is a constant drumbeat of pressure from the United States for Mexico to become more democratic, which, in my view, must happen if NAFTA is to deepen into strong integration.

When the rebellion of indigenous groups erupted on January 1, 1994, in the southern Mexican state of Chiapas, the first reaction of the Mexican authorities was to ruthlessly suppress the insurgency. Protests came from within

Mexico and from the United States as well. Congressional hearings were called to assess the state of democracy in Mexico. The U.S. reaction must have had much influence in the shift in Mexico policy from suppression of the rebellion to negotiation and mollification of the insurgents. Mexico, in this sense, lost some control over its internal affairs because the existence of NAFTA increased outside scrutiny.

The sovereignty issue also has been raised in both Canada and the United States. Many persons in the Republican Party's right wing, exemplified by Pat Buchanan, opposed NAFTA for giving Mexico too great a voice in U.S. decisions. The left wing of the Democratic Party opposed NAFTA in part because "faceless" bureaucrats – men and women from Mars, perhaps – would make too many decisions on U.S. trade and environmental policy. This argument had even more resonance when coupled with the accusation that Mexico was not a democratic country. Canada's Liberal Party, which came to power at the end of 1993, objected to provisions in both CUFTA and NAFTA that it thought compromised Canada's freedom of action in curtailing oil and gas exports to the United States during times of domestic shortage.

The more NAFTA deepens, the more sovereignty issues will be raised on such matters of protection of national industry, handling trade disputes, and protection of the environment. U.S. attention to the growth of democracy in Mexico will not diminish, particularly if NAFTA deepens. Sovereignty arguments may often be a cloak for other agendas, such as protectionism, but they are apt to find much resonance in the three countries, each of which is highly nationalistic in its own fashion.

Analysis and Opinion

This volume analyzes the foregoing issues and assesses how they should be resolved. Economic integration in North America is not taking place in isolation from developments elsewhere in the world. Even without NAFTA, the U.S. economy has become highly enmeshed with the economies of Canada and Mexico. NAFTA provides assurance of continuity within a framework of rules, but coproduction of industrial products and the provision of services has become global. This context must be understood to appreciate the significance of NAFTA and its possible extension to other countries.

U.S. corporations produce around the world. The United States is a global trader in a way that Canada and Mexico are not. These differences mean that the trade and production objectives of the three countries differ. This, too, must be understood to fully grasp the nature of the debate taking place in the respective countries.

The main chapters of this volume deal with the macro and micro decisions that must be made, of strong versus weak integration, and the potential economic consequences of deepening in North America prior to widening, or the reverse – widening and then sorting out what deepening is possible in this new arrangement. The manner in which other countries in the Western Hemisphere deal with their own subregional arrangements and with the countries of NAFTA have important repercussions for their future development, and these issues need to be analyzed.

To signal the conclusions here, I believe that deepening in North America should precede widening and that, with the possible exception of Chile, the Latin American and Caribbean countries would be well advised to strengthen their own subregional arrangements before splitting apart to seek free trade with the United States. It would be a major error in trade policy for the United States to opt for hub-and-spoke arrangements – that is, for the United States to seek free trade with other countries outside the framework of NAFTA. This brief book is designed to justify these conclusions.

2

Global Trends

To comprehend what is driving U.S. trade and investment policy requires an understanding of simultaneous developments occurring in investment, production, and trade. World exports grew more during the past decade than world production, indicating increased international interdependence (see table 2-1). The growth in trade was made possible by improvements in transportation and communication networks, but also by the steady reduction of trade barriers. The successive rounds of negotiations in GATT have been important in stimulating world trade, and, in turn, the growing importance of exports explains why so much time and effort was devoted to concluding the Uruguay Round to further reduce trade barriers.

World foreign direct investment (FDI) increased over the past decade at an even faster rate than exports (table 2-1). Production has spread to an extent hardly imaginable when the structure of international economic institutions was established at the end of World War II. FDI serves many purposes, among them to produce goods for local, regional, and global markets; to coproduce goods under which intermediate products move across borders to final assembly in different locations; and to provide services, many of a highly sophisticated nature, such as data transmission. FDI's growing importance explains why the main investment-sending countries insisted on including the

TABLE 2-1
Growth in World Direct Investment, Trade, and
Production, 1983–1989
(current values)

	Compound Annual Growth (percent)
Foreign direct investment	28.9
Exports	9.4
Gross domestic product	7.8

Source: United Nations Centre on Transnational Corporation, World
Investment Report 1991 (New York: United Nations, 1991), 4.

theme of trade-related investment measures (TRIMs) in the
Uruguay Round. This subject had not been dealt with previously in any meaningful way in GATT. The increasing
trade in intermediate products – the production of inputs in
one or many locations and their final assembly in still other
places – also explains the desire for low border barriers.
The higher these barriers, the more costly such a world
coproduction strategy would be.

Both these phenomena – the greater growth of FDI as
compared with merchandise exports and the greater
growth of exports as compared with world production –
are driving developments in the global economy. In addition to the increase in merchandise exports, there also has
been increased trade in services. This theme and TRIMs
were the main "new" issues in the Uruguay Round – but
only in the negotiating sense. Including them in GATT
ensures openness and provides guidelines for disciplinary
measures. The negotiations were a way of catching up with
real developments on the world scene. It is sometimes said
that because of the growth of regionalism and bilateralism,
GATT is dead. Yet this argument ignores the need for
greater predictability and discipline in the conduct of
global trade and investment, in each case in both goods
and services.

TABLE 2-2
Trade within and between Three World Regions, 1980
and 1990
(percent merchandise imports, current values)

	1980	1990
Trade within regions		
European Community (EC)	48	59
North America	35	46
East Asia	36	42
Trade between regions		
North America-EC	10[a]	9[a]
North America-East Asia	19	16
EC-East Asia	11	13

Sources: U.S. Department of Commerce; Eurostat, *Analytical Tables of Foreign Trade*; Ippei Yamazawa, "Japan's Future Trade and Investment Policies in the Western Hemisphere," paper prepared for a conference on the Future of Western Hemisphere Economic Integration sponsored by the Center for Strategic and International Studies, Inter-American Dialogue, and North-South Center of the University of Miami, Washington, D.C., March 2–4, 1994.

[a]Percentages based on imports of EC of 12 nations. If intra-EC trade is excluded from total imports, the percentages would be 19 percent for 1980 and 21 percent for 1990.

Alongside these global developments, however, regionalism has become a growing force in the world economy. It has now become commonplace to describe the world trading structure as divided into three main regions: Europe, particularly Western Europe; East Asia; and the Americas, particularly North America. The regions are very different, and none of them looks exclusively inward, but it is true that merchandise trade within these regions has increased more over the past decade than between them (see table 2-2). There is thus empirical evidence to support the general gut feeling voiced when NAFTA was under debate that the world was moving into a tripolar economic structure. The word "blocs" was used by those who decried this development. Even stronger pejoratives were "Fortress Europe" or "Fortress North America," but the fortress description can be justified only if intraregional trade leads to an absolute diminution of imports from outside the region—which has not been occurring. Beyond that, as table 2-2 makes clear, the alleged North American fortress is much less of a closed system than Western Europe and not much different from East Asia as measured by the respective proportions of intraregional trade.

Alongside these two simultaneous trends of increasing global interdependence and burgeoning regional economic integration, there has been movement toward what has been called "aggressive unilateralism."[1] This is typified in the United States by the growing use of contingent protection in the form of accusations that foreign companies are dumping goods in the U.S. market or enjoy unfair subsidies from their governments.[2] Unilateralism takes other forms, such as threats to curtail imports as in some way "unfair," and doing this outside the established framework of the multilateral structure embodied in GATT. The desire for greater discipline, as exemplified in the inclusion of new areas within GATT, has been accompanied by a desire to escape rigid GATT disciplines in the traditional use of safeguards against competitive merchandise imports. Although the United States is often singled out as the main culprit in fostering this duality, the practice is reasonably universal. The United States merely does it with greater transparency than most other countries.

These three tendencies—global expansion of trade and investment, even greater regional growth in trade and investment, and reactive measures of unilateralism almost as a safety valve to the increasing involvement in the international economy—are taking place simultaneously. There are inconsistencies among the three, yet they undoubtedly must coexist in the political economies of most countries, certainly in the political economy of the United States. The challenge the world faces is to make this coexistence as frictionless as possible.

What Drives U.S. Regionalism?

The trend of growing FDI and of the increasing share of exports in relation to gross domestic product applies to the United States as it does to the international economy generally. U.S. exports of goods and services reached a postwar high of 11.6 percent of GDP in 1993, compared with less than 5 percent in 1965. The goods portion of exports was 7.3 percent of GDP in 1993.[3]

The Investment Imperative

The amount of U.S. FDI increased between 1982 and 1992 from $208 billion to $487 billion, measured on a historical-cost basis. On this same basis, the FDI position in the United States was $420 billion at the end of 1992.[4] The historical-cost basis understates the current value of FDI. The Department of Commerce therefore also measures the U.S. FDI position on two other bases—current cost (the amount outstanding under this measure was $666 billion at the end of 1992) and market value ($776 billion at the end of 1992).[5]

The rapid growth of FDI into the United States has been recent, but the growth of U.S. FDI abroad has been relatively steady over a longer period. Using the historical-cost basis thus understates the position of FDI in the United States less than it does the U.S. FDI position in other countries. Even using the historical cost measure, however, FDI grew more in both directions during the decade 1982–1992 than did U.S. trade, either exports or imports, even when trade is measured in current-value terms (see table 2-3).

Most FDI, whether from the United States or other countries, is made by large, multinational corporations (MNCs). It goes without saying that MNCs, because of their size, are influential in the decision making of all market economies. Largely at their insistence, the issue of investment was taken up in GATT, and their support was

TABLE 2-3
Growth in U.S. Foreign Direct Investment
Abroad and Foreign Direct Investment in
the United States and in U.S. Exports and
Imports, 1982–1992

	Average Annual Growth (percent)
U.S. FDI abroad[a]	8.9
FDI in the U.S.[a]	12.0
U.S. exports[b]	7.5
U.S. imports[b]	8.1

Source: Russell B. Scholl, Jeffrey H. Lowe, and Sylvia
Bargas, "The International Investment Position of the
United States in 1992," *Survey of Current Business* 73,
no. 6 (June 1993): 49; and U.S. Department of Commerce.
[a]Historical-cost basis.
[b]Current values.

crucial for the negotiation and approval of NAFTA by the
United States. Opponents of the agreement criticized
NAFTA as having more to do with investment than with
trade. Mexican opponents were concerned about foreign
domination of significant Mexican industries and financial
institutions.[6] U.S. opponents, particularly in the labor
movement, argued that although NAFTA provided benefits to MNCs, it offered nothing to working men and
women. Ross Perot's "giant sucking sound" was directed at
the fear that U.S. corporations would hollow out the U.S.
manufacturing base in search of cheap labor in Mexico.

Yet the separation of trade and investment by NAFTA
critics does not stand up to careful scrutiny. Goods shipped
by U.S. parent companies to affiliates and unaffiliated foreigners were $262 billion in 1991, or 62 percent of all U.S.
merchandise exports. Of these, $108 billion (44 percent)
were shipped to majority-owned affiliates. U.S. merchan-

dise imports associated with MNCs amounted to $216 billion in 1991, or 44 percent of all imports.[7] The evidence is overwhelming that trade and investment go together.

The same reinforcement of trade is evident when foreign MNCs invest in the United States. In 1991, U.S. affiliates of foreign companies accounted for 23 percent of U.S. merchandise exports and 37 percent of U.S. imports. This trade of foreign affiliates accounted for more than 50 percent of the U.S. merchandise trade deficit that year.[8] Foreigners invest here and then ship more goods into the United than they export from the United States, just as U.S. overseas investors export more from home than they import from foreign countries.

The evidence presented is counterintuitive. The AFL-CIO resisted approval of NAFTA because of its conviction that business would flee the United States to take advantage of low wages in Mexico, and this argument found much resonance in the general public. Ralph Nader set forth his own variant of this theme when he offered the most important tool against what he called this "corporate blackmail": "Go abroad. Only you are not going to be able to sell back in this country if you play that game."[9]

Yet that vision is surreal, and certainly outdated. Putting together a single final product may involve manufacture of intermediate goods in many locations. An automobile is not produced solely in the United States. Parts come from many countries, including Mexico and Canada. A computer has sophisticated insides, à la Intel, but the assembly of labor-intensive parts may take place in Mexico, Central America, the Caribbean, or wherever. U.S. textiles move to many locations for the fabrication of products. If Nader had his way—if the output of foreign affiliates of U.S. corporations were kept out of the United States—then the shipment of intermediate goods to the foreign affiliates by the U.S. parents would not take place either. Based on the evidence, there would then be a greater curtailment of U.S. exports than of imports.

There may be a disconnect, however, in that the U.S.

workers who produce the export products are unlikely to be the same as those who face competition and even loss of jobs from the imports. But this is a separate issue from the effects of U.S. FDI on total U.S. exports. The country owes some compensation in the form of extended benefits or retraining to those who are adversely affected by foreign trade, but not at the price of sacrificing the jobs of others who benefit from these increased exports. For the most part, the export jobs generated by U.S. FDI are higher paying than the jobs that may be lost as a result of the increased imports. Keeping out these foreign goods, therefore, would involve a tradeoff of sacrificing superior jobs in order to retain inferior jobs.

Even the basic assumption that MNCs are prone to flee from the United States to seek lower wages cannot be demonstrated because overseas manufacturing operations tend to be located in high-wage, not low-wage countries. In addition, the Department of Commerce concludes from its analysis of U.S. MNCs that "overall, the growth of MOFA's (majority-owned foreign affiliates) producing in low-wage countries for the U.S. market does not appear to be associated with significant substitution of foreign for domestic employment by U.S. MNC's."[10]

The pattern of production described here—coproduction under which parts of final products are made in more than one location—is not unique to the United States. As its wage levels increased, Japanese firms resorted to coproduction with countries in East Asia. The Japanese sought to retain the sophisticated, high-valued-added activities at home in order to support a high-wage economy, and this is precisely what Europeans and Americans are doing as well.

The value of such coproduction with Mexico and Canada has the same logic for U.S. corporations as it does in East Asia for Japanese corporations. Geographic proximity it can reduce transportation costs, which explains the attraction of the Mexican border for coproduction. And because U.S. companies have long been active in the two neighboring countries, they are more familiar with their business and cultural habits than they are in places where this long experience is lacking.

U.S. FDI in Canada at the end of 1992 was $68 billion, on a historical-cost basis, or 14 percent of all U.S. FDI. The figures for Mexico were $13 billion, or a little more than 2.5 percent.[11] U.S. FDI in Canada is larger than in any country other than the United Kingdom, and U.S. FDI in Mexico is larger than in any developing country save Brazil. At the same time, U.S. merchandise exports to Canada are greater than to any other country, and U.S. exports to Mexico are greater than to any other developing country. FDI and exports are not substitutes; they are complements.

Can this type of coproduction be reversed? This, in essence, is what Nader and others who agree with his thinking are advocating. Perhaps it can through a new form of protective isolation. But there would be a heavy price in terms of added consumer costs and the sacrifice of those good jobs that are generated by U.S. FDI and related exports. Even if the United States reverted to economic nationalism, other nations would not follow suit in their production techniques. If U.S. protection kept out their goods, they would retaliate. And even if there were no overt retaliation, their inability to earn dollars from exports to the United States would limit their ability to buy U.S. goods and services.

This discussion of coproduction of goods applies in its own way to the provision of services. The United States is increasingly an exporter of services, often of a highly sophisticated nature, in such areas as finance (banking and insurance), engineering, accounting, architecture, data transmission, videos and motion pictures, and wholesale trade. Many low-wage services are not traded—Big Macs are not traded as such. It is no accident that the United States insisted that NAFTA as well as GATT include freedom to trade in services as well as in goods. After all, U.S. exports of services were 4.3 percent of GDP in 1993, a proportion likely to grow in the future, just as the service sector has grown in the United States. As is the case with trade in goods, perhaps even more so, the export of services requires FDI.

There is no costless way to get off the world.

Why Mexico and Canada?

There is a logic to regional arrangements for integrating production and trade, as is evident in the dominance of Canada and Mexico in U.S. FDI among developed and developing countries. This buildup occurred before NAFTA. A similar emphasis shows up in U.S. exports. Canada is the largest market by far for U.S. exports. It took more than $100 billion of U.S. exports in 1993, or more than 21 percent of U.S. merchandise exports to all destinations. Japan, in second place, took $48 billion. And right after Japan, in third place, Mexico took almost $42 billion of U.S. merchandise exports, or 9 percent of the total.

Detailed data on the composition of U.S. merchandise exports by country are available for 1992. In that year, $34 billion of U.S. exports to Mexico were manufactured goods, or 85 percent of all U.S. exports to Mexico. Japan, by contrast, took only $30 billion of U.S. exports classified as manufactures, or only 63 percent of U.S. merchandise exports to that country.

Manufactured exports are stressed only because they generally have more domestic value added than resource exports. They also are the main ingredients in the coproduction arrangements that are growing in regional and even in world trade. Opponents of NAFTA criticized the agreement on the ground that Mexico is too poor a country to receive large amounts of U.S. exports. The data contradict this. Those who discount the trade data also contend that much of the manufactured exports are intermediate goods intended for further elaboration in Mexico and then reshipment back to the United States. The charge is accurate, but it still required U.S. workers, in U.S. plants, to produce these intermediate products. This charge then boils down to the contention that all phases of production of manufactured goods should take place in the United States. It then becomes a non sequitur: if Mexico could not earn dollars and other foreign exchange from its own exports, it could not take as many goods of any type from the United States, intermediate or final products.

The per capita income of a country is an important determinant of its imports, as is evident from the large U.S. exports to Canada, Japan, and countries of the European Union. Canada's GDP per capita in U.S. dollars measured in the normal way of converting from Canadian dollars using the average exchange rate for the year is now about $21,000. Mexico's comparable figure as measured this way is just a little more than $3,000 a year.[12] Mexico's per capita GDP, measured on the basis of purchasing power parity, was somewhat higher, more than $5,000 in 1988, and even higher today.[13]

In any event, one conclusion drawn from looking at the high value of U.S. exports to Mexico despite its relatively low income is how much more extensive the U.S.-Mexico trade relationship would be if Mexican incomes were higher. To the extent that NAFTA contributes to raising Mexican incomes, this represents a net plus for U.S. producers and workers.

Comparing Regional Groupings

Although the evidence does show that trade within the major world regions has been growing faster than overall trade—that there is a definite regional aspect to world trade—it does not follow that all regional integration schemes are the same. The differences make comparisons risky, but this not mean that aspects of particular schemes cannot be adapted elsewhere.

One area of similarity is that a successful regional scheme, one that increases internal trade among the members by more than it increases imports from nonmembers, makes that scheme an ineluctable object for admission from outsiders. This happened to the original European Economic Community (EEC) of 6, which now numbers 12 – soon to be 16 when four members of EFTA enter – and which could possibly widen well beyond to countries in Eastern Europe. North American economic integration started with two countries under CUFTA and is now three under NAFTA. The nature of the current discussion in the Americas is who comes next and under what conditions.

The reason for this pressure toward enlargement is straightforward. Free trade areas and customs unions involve discrimination against nonmembers that takes the form of preferential tariffs and nontariff measures for members. Even under open regionalism, when border barriers are low, there are preferences for members in government procurement, techniques for rapid dispute settlement, often favored investment provisions, and rules of origin in a free trade area that favor members. Even when these are minimal – and they are not in many areas in NAFTA – decisions are taken by members that affect them and nonmembers alike. Thus, despite free trade with the EU, four members of EFTA decided they wanted to be on the inside. They also wanted a voice as regulations are written, product standards determined, and dispute-settlement techniques are devised. Mexico, when it suggested free trade negotiations with the United States, wanted to be on the inside when decisions on made on the rules of origin or to obtain recourse to a review mechanism when the United States imposed ADs or CVDs.

It is thus relevant to examine how the EU handled the question of enlargement to see how this affected progress in carrying out the basic agreement and ask what lessons might be carried over into NAFTA as the inevitable requests for membership come in. The EU devised techniques to minimize harm to other European countries either unready or unwilling to join, and there may be lessons here as well for NAFTA.

The first objective of the EU was to establish a customs union – that is, to set a common external tariff (CET) for all its members. The CET was but one aspect of what was intended to be a common commercial policy. To further this objective, the EC Commission, the EU's secretariat, negotiated trade agreements on the EU's behalf—for example, in GATT.

The Treaty of Rome, establishing the predecessor to the EU, also envisaged free movement of factors of production, capital, and labor. The phrase "common market" is used to describe this aspiration. Other than the movement of Germans from the East to the West after unification—and at that point, this became migration within a single country—there has not been extensive migration between EU countries. In fact, migration within NAFTA, from Mexico to the United States, both legal and undocumented, has been more substantial than within the EU. But the EU principle remains—it is to be a common market, with free movement of labor, and this provision may one day have great salience. NAFTA quite consciously excluded migration, at U.S. insistence.[14]

Following approval of the Maastricht Treaty, the EU now contemplates reaching economic and monetary union (EMU) by the turn of the century. This may be delayed, or perhaps never take place, but the record of accomplishing ever-increasing deepening of the EU should make observers wary of predicting failure. The ultimate goal of political union is more distant and more problematic.

NAFTA does not contemplate many of these objectives. There is no expectation that there will be either monetary or economic union in North America. There is no parliament in NAFTA, as there is in the EU. There is no court of justice in NAFTA, as there is in the EU. Perhaps, most critical, NAFTA has a minimal secretariat, one that does not have the authority to propose initiatives, as is the case in the EU. The EU set up a structure designed to enmesh the member countries in a variety of economic relations, and ultimately political relations, whereas the NAFTA idea was to minimize these derogations from sovereignty.

The grand strategy of the founding fathers of the EU was to so intertwine economic relations among the member countries – France and Germany in particular – as to make conflict unthinkable. This strategy has succeeded. NAFTA, on the other hand, was conceived as an economic agreement. War between the United States and either Canada or Mexico was already unthinkable. The difference in power relationships made this so, even apart from the longer peaceful period in North American than in Europe. When Canada entered into its integration movement with the United States, the free trade area format was chosen deliberately as having less political content than a customs union – that is, no CET and no common commercial policy.

Yet, the differences are not necessarily as profound as they appear to be on the surface. To obtain a close and cooperative economic relationship in NAFTA, Mexico found itself obliged to change its rhetoric toward the United States. Campaign speeches from candidates of the dominant party, the Institutional Revolutionary Party (PRI), shifted away from what had been a heavy overlay of anti-Americanism. Coordination on foreign policy issues – for example, in the United Nations – replaced what seemed earlier to be visceral opposition to most U.S. positions. Political union between Mexico and the United States is not in prospect, but greater political cooperation is already evident. NAFTA has its own political content.

NAFTA does not contemplate monetary union, but it surely will spawn greater monetary coordination. This has already occurred. The permanent establishment in the spring of 1994 of a $6 billion swap line between the central banks of the United States and Mexico, plus the opening by Canada of its own swap line with Mexico, is evidence of this. The purpose of this line of credit is to provide resources, if necessary, to minimize fluctuations in exchange-rate relationships. The more countries trade, the less volatility they want in their exchange rates with respect to each other. The EU started this way as well. Although not monetary union, it is monetary cooperation.

The issue of separate external tariffs is also somewhat overdone. Any NAFTA country that retains a significantly higher tariff on imports from outside the region for capital and intermediate goods will disadvantage its own industries that need these imports. Investors will have an incentive to go to the lower tariff country. There will thus be much pressure for tariffs to unify for goods required for further production. There will even be pressure for comparable tariffs on consumer goods. Canada learned to its chagrin that raising cigarette taxes well above the U.S. level spawned contraband to exploit the difference. This will apply to many other consumer goods as well.

NAFTA has a skeletal secretariat as compared with the EU. In addition, program and policy suggestions in NAFTA will have to come from the governments themselves. This is true in the EU as well, but there the Commission has considerable independent authority to make proposals. The ideas of completing the common market under EC-92 (removing the remaining internal barriers to trade by the end of 1992) and then reaching EMU by the end of the century came from the Commission. The EU Commission is also quite elaborate; it acts as the executive arm of the Union, replete with senior officials who have the equivalent of cabinet rank.

The NAFTA countries deliberately chose a less bureaucratic arrangement. There is an abhorrence of establishing new institutions in the U.S. executive branch and the Congress, and although the Free Trade Commission is a new institution, its personnel and authority are minimal. The NAFTA Commission, the name given the cabinet officials from the three countries who nominally run NAFTA, can make suggestions for new actions and meet to settle disputes.[15]

The question of a Commission with greater authority and a larger staff may arise in the future if NAFTA is expanded to other countries. In that case, the minimal arrangements that now exist may be inadequate for coordinating activities among many countries; what is suitable for three countries becomes less viable as the number rises to four, five, or more. The greater the number of countries, the more discrepancies in interpretation of the agreement are likely to arise. This issue is discussed at greater length in chapter 5 on the possible widening of NAFTA.

The lack of a powerful commission with an independent staff does not mean that NAFTA lacks institutional structure. An annex to chapter 20 of the agreement lists eight committees and working groups dealing with trade in goods, worn clothing, agriculture, sanitary measures, standards, small business, financial services, and private commercial disputes. Several of these committees have subcommittees or advisory bodies. Other working groups have already been established to consider rules of origin, customs procedures, transportation regulations, and other functions.

The various dispute-settlement provisions of the agreement call for establishing rosters of panelists to arbitrate trade and investment conflicts. The supplemental agreements to NAFTA establish two other commissions, one for environmental cooperation to be located in Montreal and another for labor cooperation, to be located in Dallas, Texas. (The Free Trade Commission will be situated in Mexico City.) Each of these has its own subbodies. There is a border environmental group. To help finance border infrastructure and environmental projects, a North American Development Bank (NADBank) will be headquartered in San Antonio, Texas. It is designed to use government guaranties to facilitate borrowing from private capital markets.

Latin American and Caribbean Integration Arrangements

Latin America and the Caribbean are replete with their own subregional integration schemes that differ from each other and from either NAFTA or the EU. Some have a rather elaborate institutional structure, such as the Andean group of countries (Bolivia, Colombia, Ecuador, Peru, and Venezuela), while others are more akin in their structure to NAFTA–for example, MERCOSUR (the Southern Cone Common Market, consisting of Argentina, Brazil, Paraguay, and Uruguay). In addition to these two subregional groupings, there is the Central American Common Market (CACM), made up of Costa Rica, El Salvador, Guatemala, Honduras, and Nicaragua, as well as the Caribbean Community and Common Market (CARICOM), with 13 members. Eight CARICOM countries have their own subregional grouping, the Organization of Eastern Caribbean States (OECS). Over and above these subregional economic groupings, the Latin American Integration Association (ALADI, from its initials in Spanish) has 11 members, almost all of which are members of one or another of the subregional groups.

This is by no means the end of the complexity of subregional economic groupings in the Americas. Mexico, a member of NAFTA, has free trade agreements with Chile and Costa Rica, the latter a member of CACM. Mexico, Colombia, and Venezuela (the G-3) have entered into their own free trade arrangement even though Colombia and Venezuela are both members of the Andean group. Colombia has also stated that it wishes to negotiate for accession into NAFTA. Argentina, a member of MERCOSUR, has indicated its interest in acceding to NAFTA if it can work out its relations with Brazil. Brazil has suggested establishing a South American Free Trade Area as a substitute for NAFTA for the countries of that large subregion.

Latin America and the Caribbean have long histories of wider, subregional economic integration. These arrangements were promoted in the 1950s and 1960s by the Economic Commission for Latin America (ECLA) as a way to widen the area for the import-substitution policies then practiced throughout the region. These schemes failed. The current effort approaches integration under largely open markets following unilateral reductions in tariff and nontariff barriers by practically all the countries.

The current model is what ECLAC (the old ECLA with the addition of the Caribbean) has called "open regionalism."[16] It is this shift from regional integration behind high barriers, which is tantamount to protectionism rather than trade liberalization, to economic integration behind low import barriers that makes the current prospects for subregional integration within Latin America and the Caribbean and for affiliation with NAFTA so promising.

Conclusion

The trend toward regional cohesion is extremely strong, even as global economic interaction is growing. Regionalism has taken its most comprehensive form in Europe. Integration in North America also is quite ambitious in that it deals with much more than trade, but it is far less comprehensive in its structure or ultimate objectives than in Europe. Although no formal structure links Japan with the other countries of East Asia, integration is in fact taking place in trade, investment, and production relations. A similar trend, but on a smaller scale, is occurring in Latin America and the Caribbean, and trade and investment within that region also have been growing.

The trend toward economic cohesion in many geographic areas is driven by the same fundamental considerations, although there are idiosyncrasies by region. The common underlying features are the growing role of investment; coproduction of parts of final products in the most desirable location depending on geography, resources, wages, and enlarging markets. All the integration schemes mentioned have preferential elements relating to tariffs, nontariff measures, government procurement, and other aspects, except that in East Asia between Japan and other countries, but the pattern is largely that of "open regionalism."[17]

Clearly integration is not driven merely, or even significantly, by tariff preferences. This point merits some elaboration in view of the oft-used argument that NAFTA, or any other agreement under open regionalism, is not necessary because tariffs are already so low. What these agreements do is formalize continuity of treatment. President Carlos Salinas of Mexico, for example, wanted NAFTA to limit the option of any successor to regress to a model of high protectionism. When Jean Chrétien and Canada's Liberal Party succeeded the Conservatives in running the Canadian government at the end of 1993, the choice was to continue NAFTA despite much Liberal Party opposition when both CUFTA and NAFTA were conceived. The existence of a formal agreement does not necessarily lock in its terms, but makes radical policy change infinitely more difficult. Too many interests are developed in the new policy to dismiss it cavalierly. Businesspersons are thereby assured of more predictable treatment.

But there is an even deeper point as to why countries with low tariffs enter into economic integration agreements. Economic relations depend on so many considerations other than trade. Countries care about investment rules; they want reasonable predictability in setting industrial, health, and safety standards; they seek techniques to avoid surprises in national regulations; they wish some reasonable consistency in tax burdens made necessary by the footloose nature of production; they look to their central banks and treasuries to do what they can to minimize exchange-rate volatility; and they welcome consultation on seemingly mundane issues – customs procedures, rules of origin, trucking regulations, et cetera; they are the grease that make the machine of economic integration function smoothly.

Modern free trade agreements are about trade, to be sure, but they also deal more broadly with economic relations between countries. The European Economic Community was better named than the North American Free Trade Agreement. One only has to look at the chapter headings of NAFTA to realize how extensive are its understandings: trade in goods comes first, but then come chapter headings like technical barriers to trade, government procurement, investment, trade in services, telecommunications, financial services, competition policy, temporary entry for businesspersons, and intellectual property. NAFTA's supplemental agreements even go beyond to cover the environment and labor. This comprehensiveness of NAFTA – of modern integration agreements – has much relevance to the expansion of NAFTA, a theme taken up in chapter 5.

3

Economic Interaction in North America

The two U.S. land borders are busy places. Of the 483 million legal admissions into the United States reported by the Immigration and Naturalization Service (INS) for fiscal year 1993, more than 269 million entered overland from Mexico and another 132 million by land from Canada. The two borders together accounted for 83 percent of all admissions. (All the figures include entry of both U.S. citizens and aliens.) In addition, U.S. immigration authorities apprehended 1.3 million illegal aliens in fiscal year 1993, and practically all this activity took place at or near the border with Mexico.

At least 1.7 million trucks crossed the U.S.-Mexico border in both directions in 1993. Southbound surface traffic of goods in 1989 was 21 million tons, three quarters of which went through Laredo, Texas; northbound surface tonnage was 16 million, which moved through two main ports of entry, Laredo (42 percent) and Nogales (27 percent, largely fruits and vegetables).[1] One major trucking firm states that the average delay for trucks coming from Nuevo Laredo and crossing into the United States at Laredo, just across the border, is 12 hours. Such delay is the result of a shortage of bridges, the search for drugs and illegal aliens, and burdensome and inadequately coordinated customs procedures between Mexico and the United States. These figures, which are pre-NAFTA, are certain to increase as the United States and Mexico forge closer economic and cultural relations.

The U.S. population, based on 1990 census data, is 9 percent Hispanic origin (Hispanic is the word the U.S. Census Bureau uses, although many scholars prefer the word Latino), and about 60 percent of that is of Mexican origin (or 5.4 percent of the total U.S. population). Between 1980 and 1990, the overall Hispanic population grew by 53 percent, and the subgroup of Mexican-origin population grew by 54 percent, while the overall U.S. population grew by only 10 percent. The black population grew by 13 percent over that period, and there is no doubt that the Hispanic population will soon be the largest U.S. minority. California is already 34 percent Hispanic and Texas 19 percent, and the Hispanics in these two border states are almost exclusively of Mexican origin.

Neighborhood counts. At the southern border with Mexico, this influence has led to a complex Mexicanization of the United States and Americanization of Mexico. For a variety of reasons—history, the proximity of a rich and a developing country, the reinforcing nature of kinship—the U.S. Southwest looks south. By the same token, U.S. cultural habits are affecting Mexico, an influence felt more on that country's northern border—where the closest business relations exist with the United States—than anywhere else. Because of family and economic relations and the mixing of cultures, the people of northern Mexico look north almost as much as they look south to Mexico City. It is at the border that the environmental problems of the two nations collide. It was at the border that the *maquiladora* phenomenon erupted.

Policy makers and pundits often play a game of ranking countries in terms of their importance to the United States. Great Britain always ranked high because of the original U.S. heritage. So does the rest of Europe. The Soviet Union was undoubtedly priority number one during the cold war, and Russia still holds a high rank, but not quite like before. China must rank high if only on population grounds, but also because of the presence of overseas

Chinese plus China's recent economic growth. India for some reason has never ranked high in U.S. policy terms, despite its large population, but this will change as India's economy is strengthened. As a successful book—*Japan as Number One* by Ezra Vogel—once proclaimed, Japan would one day emerge as the world's leading power because of its economic achievements, replacing the United States.

Although neither Mexico nor Canada has figured as a number one in U.S. policy, the situation is now changing. What happens in a neighboring country, particularly a populous one like Mexico, affects the United States more directly than what happens far away. U.S. ethnicity is being altered before our eyes, a change hardly noticed until recently. Is Mexico number one? Perhaps. At least it should enter into consideration.

The discussion that follows deals with trade relations in North America, with some side commentary on U.S. trade throughout the Americas and on factor movements in North America—that is, of capital and labor.

U.S. Trade in North America

Table 3-1 shows how important the Americas are in global U.S. merchandise exports. In trade relations, the United States is not Europe-centered, but it is Americas-centered. If Asian economic growth rates continue to be high, as they have been in recent decades, the two areas—the Americas and Asia—will dwarf Europe in trade importance for the United States.

Table 3-2 shows the importance of neighborhood in trade relations in the Americas. The United States in 1993, as in earlier years, shipped more goods to Canada than to the rest of the Americas put together. Canada has a population of roughly 27 million; the rest of the hemisphere, according to the Inter-American Development Bank, has a population of about 450 million, 17 times as great. U.S. exports clearly are not determined merely by

TABLE 3-1
Direction of U.S. Merchandise
Exports by Region, 1993
(current values)

	Percent
Western Hemisphere	38
Asia	28
Europe	26
Other	7
	100

Source: Author's calculation from U.S. Department of Commerce, Economics and Statistics Administration, Bureau of the Census, "U.S. Merchandise Trade: December 1993," p. 18.

Note: Totals may not add due to rounding; data are preliminary.

the population size of market destinations; income levels play a role as do the economic relationships built up over the years.

Table 3-2 also shows that if Canada is excluded from the count, the United States in 1993 shipped more goods to Mexico than to the rest of the Americas. In this case, the roughly 88 million people of Mexico receive more U.S. goods than do the remaining 360 million people in other countries of the hemisphere. This has less to do with per capita income – Mexico is not a high income country – than with proximity, the extent of U.S. investment in Mexico, and the changes in Mexican economic policy since the mid-1980s.[2]

From the low point in 1986 (when U.S. merchandise exports to Mexico were not much more than $12 billion), through 1993 (when U.S. exports to Mexico were almost $42 billion), the average annual rate of increase in exports was 19 percent.[3] Imports from Mexico also increased over

TABLE 3-2
U.S. Merchandise Exports to the
Western Hemisphere, 1993
(current values)

	Billions of dollars	Percent
Canada	100	56
Mexico	42	24
Brazil	6	3
Venezuela	5	3
Argentina	4	2
Colombia	3	2
Other	18	10
	178	100

Source: Author's calculating from U.S. Department of Commerce, "U.S. Merchandise Trade: December 1993," p. 18.
Note: Data are preliminary.

this period, from $17 billion in 1986 to $40 billion in 1993, or at an annual average rate of less than 13 percent. The low level of U.S. exports in 1986 can be explained by the economic depression that still gripped Mexico, plus the largely closed nature of the economy. The growth in U.S. exports since then can be understood by economic recovery, even though this has been relatively modest averaging about 2.5 percent a year since 1986, and also the shift in policy opening the Mexico economy to imports.

Much was made during the NAFTA debate by U.S. proponents that Mexico is one of the few countries with which the United States has a substantial surplus in trade in goods; this argument was coupled with the turnaround in the U.S. trade balance with Mexico, from deficit in the mid-1980s to surplus in the 1990s. A trade surplus, however, is a slim reed on which to base support for economic integration. The more important measure is the growth in total trade in both directions because this is what creates economic activity and jobs. And this growth has been nothing less than phenomenal. It can continue only if the two countries maintain reasonably high growth rates. U.S. merchandise exports to Mexico grew by only 2.5 percent in 1993, a year in which Mexico had practically no economic growth, much lower than in the earlier years when the Mexican economy turned around.

The U.S. share of Mexico's merchandise imports has been in the 60 to 70 percent range for decades. Mexico imports a minimum of $800 million more in merchandise for each 1 percent increase in GDP, and U.S. exporters secure more than $500 million of this. The richer Mexico becomes, the more trade will take place with the United States to the benefit of both.

The Canadian situation is similar to Mexico's in that the United States captures between 60 to 70 percent of Canada's far larger imports. There is thus what might be called a natural economic integration relationship in North America for the United States. The word "natural" may be too mechanical in that what is now taken for granted had first to be created over many years.

The logic of Western Hemisphere free trade also rests in part on the dominant role of the United States in exporting to countries in this hemisphere. For the hemisphere as a whole, excluding Canada and Mexico, the United States is the beneficiary of about 40 percent of hemispheric imports, although the precise percentage varies from year to year. By contrast, U.S. exporters capture only between 15 and 25 percent of European and Asian markets. There may thus be some offsetting advantages for developing closer economic relations in the Western Hemisphere compared with, say, Asia. Asian growth rates are higher, making them more attractive markets for imports from all sources, but the United States obtains a greater share of the imports that are generated by growth in Latin America.

Yet the ratio declines the further south one goes in Latin America. Once again, neighborhood counts. The U.S. proportion of country imports is about 50 percent for Central America and the Caribbean, closer to 40 percent for Colombia and Venezuela, and around 10 to 25 percent in the southern cone of Argentina, Brazil, and Chile. In this sense, only a few hemispheric countries constitute the kind of natural market for the United States that exists in Canada and Mexico. What also matters, however, is future potential for the market development of the kind that has taken place in North America. Although most countries of the Western Hemisphere are not now the natural market for the United States that Canada and Mexico are, they can be converted into that.

U.S. merchandise exports to the countries of the Western Hemisphere other than Canada are predominantly manufactured goods. Based on data from the U.S. Department of Commerce, manufactures accounted for $64 billion out of a total of $76 billion of U.S. exports to these countries in 1992, or 84 percent. Nine of the ten leading U.S. commodity exports to these countries in 1992 were manufactures (see table 3-3).

Manufactured commodities, by contrast, comprised $41 billion of total U.S. imports of $69 billion in 1992 from the developing countries of the Western Hemisphere, or 60 percent. Four of the ten leading commodity imports from these countries were primary products, and oil alone accounted for 20 percent of all imports (see table 3-4).

Although there is nothing necessarily superior about exporting manufactures rather than primary products, they do incorporate more value added. Tables 3-3 and 3-4 together show the comparative advantages that currently prevail in U.S. trade alongside the comparative advantages that favor the United States in manufactures and the other countries in primary products. But there is substantial trade in both types of products in both directions.

Investment Relations

U.S. foreign direct investment is substantial in Canada and still quite modest in Mexico, at least as measured on a

TABLE 3-3
Ten Leading Items in U.S. Merchandise Exports to Developing Countries in the Western Hemisphere, 1992

Commodity	Billions of Dollars
Motor vehicle parts	4.5
Aircraft equipment	3.3
Various low-value manufactures, not identified by kind	2.6[a]
Telecommunications equipment	2.4
Noncrude oil from petroleum and bituminous minerals	1.9
Automatic data processing machines	1.7
Engineering plant and equipment	1.7
Electrical machinery	1.6
Internal combustion engines	1.4
Parts for office machinery	1.4

Source: U.S. Department of Commerce, International Trade Administration, Office of Trade and Economic Analysis, *U.S. Foreign Trade Highlights, 1992* (Washington, D.C.: U.S. Government Printing Office, 1993), 126.

[a]This is a catchall item whose accuracy is suspect.

historical-cost basis (see table 3-5). In fact, U.S. FDI is higher in Canada than in any other country except the United Kingdom where the large figure is an artifact of substantial investments in banking and finance. These funds make up almost half of U.S. FDI in the UK and do not necessarily show up in productive investment in the UK itself. This situation is, in part, similar to the U.S. FDI in Bermuda and Panama shown in table 3-5. By contrast, as table 3-4 shows, all but 20 percent of U.S. FDI in Canada is outside the banking and finance sector (see table 3-4).

What is interesting in the case of Mexico is the high proportion—70 percent—of U.S. direct investment in manufacturing (see table 3-6). This reflects the large role of coproduction undertaken by U.S. companies, particularly

TABLE 3-4
Ten Leading Items in U.S. Merchandise Imports from Developing Countries in the Western Hemisphere, 1992

Commodity	Billions of Dollars
Crude oil	10.8
Noncrude oil from petroleum and bituminous minerals	4.7
Motor cars and other vehicles	2.7
Parts and accessories of motor vehicles	2.3
Equipment for distributing electricity	2.1
Fruits and nuts	2.0
Special commodities not classified by kind	1.9
Footwear	1.6
Men's or boys' coats and jackets	1.5
Coffee	1.4

Source: U.S. Department of Commerce, *U.S. Foreign Trade Highlights, 1992*, p. 127.

in maquiladora plants. The word "maquiladora" is by now well known. It refers to the procedure by which parts of products are produced in the United States or some other foreign country, then shipped to Mexico for further elaboration. The resulting product is usually shipped back to the United States, and the tariff is imposed only on the value added outside the United States. The treatment of imports under this type of production sharing falls under provisions 9802.00.60 and 9802.00.80 of the harmonized tariff schedule. These provisions are applied worldwide and not just to Mexico. The maquiladora will largely become an anachronism under NAFTA, as discussed below.

The low proportion of U.S. FDI in banking and finance in Mexico will most likely change as that sector opens under NAFTA. There is a potentially large market for U.S. banking, investment banking, and insurance firms in Mex-

TABLE 3-5
U.S. Direct Investment in North America, 1992
(historical-cost basis)

	Billions of Dollars	Percent of Total
Canada	68	14
Bermuda[a]	26	5
Brazil	16	3
Mexico	13	3
Panama[a]	11	2
Remaining countries in Western Hemisphere	23	5
Rest of world	330	68
Total	487	100

Source: "U.S. Direct Investment Abroad: Detail for Historical-Cost Position and Balance of Payments Flows, 1992," Survey of Current Business 73, no. 7 (July 1993): 100.

[a]These figures are not for productive direct investment in Bermuda or Panama as such, which serve as offshore facilities for handling U.S. capital flows.

ico; opening this opportunity was a major accomplishment of NAFTA.

The U.S. Department of Commerce figures for FDI in Mexico seem low, in part because of the historical-cost measurement technique. The U.S. embassy in Mexico reports the cumulative level of U.S. FDI in 1992 as $23 billion, or $10 billion more than shown in table 3-5. This represents about 60 percent of FDI in Mexico from all sources.[4]

The static FDI data presented in tables 3-5 and 3-6 also miss the dynamism of the U.S. investment relationship with Mexico since the change in Mexico's overall economic policy in the latter half of the 1980s and then the negotiation of NAFTA. U.S. and other FDI moving into Mexico was quite modest compared with similar investment going into Europe and Canada extending back over

TABLE 3-6
Sectoral Breakdown of U.S. Direct Investment in
Mexico and Canada, 1992
(percent, historical-cost basis)

	Canada	Mexico
Petroleum	12	a
Manufacturing	49	70
Wholesale trade	8	6
Banking and finance	20	6
Other services	3	2
All other	8	15
	100	99[a]

Source: "U.S. Direct Investment Abroad: Detail for Historical-Cost Position and Balance of Payments Flows, 1992," p. 100.

[a]Suppressed in original to avoid disclosure of individual companies. The amount is small as evidenced by the fact that without petroleum, total adds to 99 percent.

half a century. During the 1970s, FDI in Mexico from all sources averaged less than $600 million a year. Its peak, before the economic collapse in 1982, was less than $3 billion in 1981, and it then declined sharply after that to less than $500 million a year.[5] By contrast, FDI has been substantial in more recent years, almost $5 billion in 1991 and about $5.5 billion in 1992.

Attracting FDI was a major objective for Mexico in concluding NAFTA. This represents a sea change in Mexican thinking. Before the debt crisis that erupted in 1982, the Mexican tendency was to tolerate foreign investment and then only on its terms, or what the negotiating position would permit. The 1973 law that guided FDI represented this spirit; it was called the Law to *Promote* Mexican Investment and *Regulate* Foreign Investment (emphasis added). What Mexico and other developing countries learned from the decade of the 1980s was that they lost control over their economic destiny from accumulating too much foreign debt – perhaps even more control than if they had sought FDI instead. According to the agreement reached in NAFTA, Mexico enacted a new foreign investment law in 1993 that, with exceptions, extends national treatment to foreign investors. This law, in most respects, provides comparable conditions for investors from all countries, but there are some special features on percent of ownership in some sectors that favor investors from NAFTA countries.[6]

The direct investment, coupled with strategic alliances between firms in the United States and affiliates and partners in Mexico and Canada, generates much trade within the same industries and even within the same firms. Thus, if one looks at Canada-U.S. trade, the three most important Canadian exports are passenger automobiles, motor vehicle parts (including engines), and trucks and other motor vehicles. The two most important U.S. exports to Canada are motor vehicle parts (including engines) and passenger automobiles, and trucks and other motor vehicles rank among the first ten.[7] In assessing the trade impact of NAFTA, the U.S. International Trade Commission (USITC) concluded that the largest long-term increases in trade with Mexico would be in the automotive industry, to include export increases in both directions. The other leading items listed – computers and parts, textiles and apparel, and ceramic tile – would also show increases in both U.S. imports from and exports to Mexico.[8]

The U.S. Department of Commerce estimates that in 1991, U.S. manufactured exports to affiliates in Canada were $35 billion, or almost half of all U.S. manufactured exports to that country. U.S. exports to affiliates in Mexico were estimated at $10 billion that year, some 35 percent of manufactured exports to that country. On the import side, the comparable figures for 1991 were $36 billion from Canada, or 51 percent of manufactured imports; and $9 billion from Mexico, or 39 percent of manufactured imports from that country.[9]

These figures do not tell the full story because they estimate only trade between U.S. parent corporations and their affiliates in Canada and Mexico. Much additional trade takes place between U.S. parents and subsidiaries under various alliances, many of which are made possible because a U.S. company is directly involved in production outside the United States. Once again, the point has to be stressed: the simple equation that U.S. FDI deprives U.S. workers of employment is misleading, even false. It may deprive some U.S. workers of employment if a U.S. plant is closed to move to some other destination, but it may provide employment to other U.S. workers who will now benefit from intraindustry and intrafirm trade. In addition, this increased trade will benefit workers in the partner country. Although the evidence shows that U.S. FDI leads to a greater increase in U.S. exports than in U.S. imports, the more relevant measure is the total trade generated. This benefits all the countries concerned.

The direct investment discussion does not cover the substantial portfolio flows that have been coming to Mexico in recent years. Total capital flows into Mexico have been about $20 billion a year for the last two years, 1992 and 1993. Of this, roughly two thirds has been portfolio investment in Mexican bonds and Mexico's stock market. These flows have more than covered Mexico's deficit on current account—that is, Mexico's larger imports than exports of goods and services, plus the need to service the country's overseas debt. The large portfolio flows have, in fact, complicated Mexico's monetary policy, and much of this foreign exchange inflow has been sterilized (that is, the dollars and other foreign currencies were purchased by the Bank of Mexico, increasing Mexico's foreign reserves, and then the Bank limited monetary emission to keep down inflation).

Portfolio flows are, by their nature, volatile. They come when there is confidence in a country's economic and social stability and can leave quickly when there is uncertainty. Much of this flow is sensitive to comparative interest rates, which have been relatively high in Mexico.

The end use to which these flows have been put must also be taken into account. If investment in the Mexican stock market has served to augment productive investment, then it serves a purpose similar to direct investment. In any event, Mexico has entered the major leagues in terms of attracting foreign capital. NAFTA is designed to cement this development, but ultimately the flows depend on internal conditions in Mexico itself.

The Maquiladora Industry

The one type of FDI that aroused the most animosity in the United States, particularly among labor unions, was the establishment of maquiladora plants in Mexico. Most of these are at the border. For many years, when the major production in these plants was textile products, the overwhelming proportion of workers were women. They were badly paid, certainly by U.S. standards, and had uncertain futures in this work. Consequently, the turnover was high – frequently more than 100 percent a year.

The rationale of these plants was to carry out those parts of production that were labor-intensive in Mexico, where labor was cheap, varying between one-seventh and one-tenth of U.S. labor costs for comparable work. This was coproduction at its most basic level. The number of these plants skyrocketed during the 1980s after the peso depreciated in relation to the dollar. As a consequence, wages paid in pesos required an even lower dollar outlay. The number of maquiladora plants went from less than 600 in 1982, the year the peso went through a major devaluation, to more than 2,000 in 1992. Using Mexican data, employment in maquiladora plants was almost 500,000 at the end of 1992. Imports of parts for maquiladora plants in 1992 were almost $14 billion and exports close to $19 billion, thus leaving net exports of close to $5 billion. The $19 billion of gross maquiladora exports was 40 percent of all Mexican exports to all destinations in 1992.[10]

The composition of maquiladora exports changed over time. In 1992, exports of machinery and equipment, such as engines for motor vehicles, other auto parts, television receivers, and other consumer durables dominated all other categories. Based on U.S. data, textiles, apparel, and footwear accounted for less than 2.5 percent of the total value of imports from Mexican maquiladoras in 1992. Employment patterns also changed; the maquiladora work force became increasingly male as the product mix altered.

Although the maquiladoras have been important, they seemed destined from the start to play a transitional role in the Mexican economy. This was the experience of other countries, such as Taiwan, that started their industrial buildup with comparable export-processing zones. Well before NAFTA was in the picture, one of my publications included the comment that the best way to study the maquiladoras was as a "transition from enclave to an integral part of [Mexico's] national industrial structure."[11] NAFTA has made the elimination of maquiladora system inevitable.[12]

There are many reasons for this. One of the benefits of the structure was that U.S. tariffs paid on imports from maquiladoras were only on the value added outside the United States. This is a form of what in trade parlance is known as duty drawback; when the imports originally entered Mexico for further elaboration, they came in bond and paid no duty. These implicit drawbacks are to be phased out under NAFTA. Beyond this, NAFTA calls for zero duties on U.S. imports from Mexico to be phased in over a 10- to 15-year period. This is better treatment than the import duty on the value added. Finally, in the past there were limits on what maquiladora plants could ship into the Mexican market itself. These will be gradually eliminated and disappear by the year 2001. By then, therefore, the maquiladora plants will be part of Mexico's industrial structure.

This does not mean that the dominance of the border

for coproduction will dissipate. The border has many advantages. Its proximity to the United States simplifies
transportation problems; U.S. plant managers with families can live on the U.S. side of the border if they wish; and
there is the factor of inertia—the plants are in place. There
are advantages to shifting production inland, mainly to be
closer to the rest of Mexican industry. In addition, labor is
more scarce at the border than in other locations in Mexico.
Any shift would require upgrading Mexico's transportation and communication networks, but this will be required
in any event if NAFTA is to flourish.

One of the epithets used by opponents of NAFTA in
both the United States and Mexico is that although the
maquiladoras might disappear, NAFTA will "maquila-
dorize" all of Mexico's industry. The implication is that all
wages in Mexico will be kept low. It is just as likely, however, that integration into the Mexican industrial structure
will make the treatment of maquiladora workers similar to
that of all other workers, and industrial wages in Mexico
have not been declining in the past few years since NAFTA
expectations came on the scene. The U.S. Bureau of Labor
Statistics reports that hourly compensation for production
workers in manufacturing in Mexico rose from 11 percent
of the U.S. level in 1990, the year President Salinas suggested the idea of free trade with the United States, to 15
percent in 1992.[13]

What is happening is that the maquiladora, or export-
processing zone, technique as the entryway for production
sharing has run its course in Mexico, and the shift toward
production sharing on a broader basis is under way.
NAFTA is merely the instrument that makes this process
inevitable over a definite time frame, but it was probably
foreordained in any event.

Migration

Other than allowing for the temporary entry of businesspersons, NAFTA did not address the question of immigration because of U.S. sensitivity to any hint that NAFTA

would legalize the unlimited entry of Mexicans. The two countries were negotiating a free trade area, not a common market, which, by common usage of that term, includes free factor movement—that is, of capital and labor. The EU is a commo market; the Treaty of Rome, which established what is now the EU, contemplated free movement of labor. NAFTA included free movement of capital. Mexican critics of the agreement asked in their writings and comments why there was freedom for the one factor that the United States wanted to benefit business, but not for the other factor that many Mexicans would have preferred. This was essentially a debating point, however. Even though both are called "factors of production," labor is much more than that.

Yet the immigration issue did enter into the NAFTA debate. U.S. proponents argued that the best way to curtail the flow of undocumented immigration was to facilitate Mexico's economic development and job creation, thereby creating employment at home.[14] NAFTA opponents countered that some of the measures undertaken in NAFTA, such as removing Mexico's restrictions on corn and bean imports, would encourage outmigration from Mexico's rural areas to the cities, with a subsequent overflow into the United States. A breakdown of the votes on NAFTA's enabling legislation shows that many U.S. congressional representatives from southern California voted against the agreement, as did California's two U.S. senators.[15] The reason many of these legislators gave for voting "no" was concern about immigration from Mexico stemming from NAFTA.

Immigration has since become a hot political issue in the United States, particularly in states that receive most of the people—legal and illegal—from Mexico, Central America, and Haiti. The issue has become most incandescent in California, where the bulk of immigrants from Mexico go. California has a larger Mexican-origin population than any other state, which attracts new entrants from Mexico who wish to join families, *compadres* from their own villages, and to be in a milieu where they can merge into the general community. The clamor to "do something" about immigration has coincided with an economic slow-down in California. It was ever thus: When times are hard, anti-immigrant sentiment flourishes. California, particu-larly its fruit and vegetable growers, did not object to re-cruiting and obtaining exceptions for Mexican immigrants to harvest their crops when times were good. In fact, the 1986 immigration law had a provision to expressly encour-age such entry.

In any event, the question was joined in the NAFTA debate as to whether the agreement would lead to more illegal immigration from Mexico or less. The answer to this question revolves around the time frame considered; the short term may lead to a different outcome from the long term, even though these time frames cannot be defined precisely. A study by Philip Martin captures this duality. He concludes that NAFTA will lead to a migration hump in the 1990s because it adds to push factors in rural Mex-ico, but that the agreement is a key ingredient in eliminat-ing emigration pressures over the long term.[16] Lawrence Katz, the chief economist of the U.S. Department of Labor, made the latter point in testimony before a congressional committee: "Thus, migration will only be substantially re-duced as Mexican wage rates increase and employment op-portunities expand."[17]

Some background on the situation in Mexico can in-form this discussion. Although Mexico's rate of population increase has diminished and is today less than 2 percent a year compared with 3 to 3.5 percent as recently as three decades ago, the children from the earlier period are now either in or entering the labor force. Consequently, one part of the "hump" to which Martin referred is the growth in Mexico's labor force over the next 10 to 15 years. This is perhaps the best definition of the "long term"; a 15-year definition also coincides with the transition period to free trade in sensitive agricultural products in NAFTA.

Because of the youth of its population, Mexico must

create about 1 million new jobs a year to accommodate just the new entrants during this hump period. To provide a point of comparison, during the relatively high economic growth years of the Reagan administration, Republicans boasted about the creation of 2 million jobs a year. The population of the United States, some 250 million, is roughly three times Mexico's, which is about 88 million, and yet the United States was able to create only twice as many new jobs a year in good times as Mexico will require in what has been described here as the long term.

The Mexican job-creation task is thus formidable. Based on past relationships between overall economic growth and job creation, Mexico's economy will have to grow at about 5 to 6 percent a year to create this many jobs. It has not been growing at that rate in recent years, although the potential for such growth exists.

The relevance of this job-creation requirement is that if good jobs are not created at home, Mexicans will cross the border. U.S. usage refers to persons who enter the United States without documents as "illegal" immigrants. Yet, for the most part, they are enterprising young people with the drive to improve their lot in the world – precisely the kind of people that Mexico should not want to lose.

The short-term problem – in this context, the period from now to some 15 years into the future – is compounded by the agricultural situation in Mexico. Some 28 percent of Mexico's population live in rural areas – about 25 million people – but contribute only about 8 percent of Mexico's GDP. They are mostly poor and have every incentive to leave their farms for other locations, mainly Mexico's cities. There is no future for most of them remaining in Mexico's impoverished rural areas. Their incomes are low, their prospects dismal, and the educational opportunities for their children second-rate. Millions of these rural residents grow corn, one of Mexico's staple foods, mostly for their own consumption.

The issue, therefore, is not whether Mexico can "keep 'em down on the farm." Mexico cannot, any more than the

United States and other now industrialized countries could. The issue is the speed with which they leave and the job opportunities for them in urban areas of Mexico. The concern is that Mexico will not be able in the short term to find jobs at home for those migrating out of the country-side and, therefore, many will cross over illegally into the United States. Several respected researchers using a computable general equilibrium (CGE) model estimated the overflow of migrants into the United States as a result of NAFTA will be about 610,000.[18] The analysis did not take into account subsequent changes in Mexican agricultural policy.

In 1993, Mexico adopted a new policy called *Procampo*. Its main elements are to eliminate Mexico's current price-support system, which fixes domestic prices, particularly for corn, well above world levels, and to compensate for this change with income-support payments made directly to eligible producers. These income supports will be fixed in real terms for 10 years and then be phased out in years 11 through 15. The rationale for the shift is that current price supports, which are based on products delivered to the market and not those used for home consumption, has benefited mainly the larger producers, those who have irrigated land and do not have to rely on rainfall, as do small landholders. The argument in favor of the change is to target support payments to those farmers who need them most.

One of the main purposes of the income-support program is to encourage farmers to stay put for at least as long as the program continues. That might give time to allow the growth-generating aspects of NAFTA to take effect.

Because the high price supports raised the price of corn products, such as tortillas, consumer subsidies were also given in urban areas. Here again, the system provided little to subsistence producers in the countryside. This combination of producer and consumer subsidies imposed a high burden on the Mexican budget. The expectation is that without the price-support program, corn and other agricultural product prices in Mexico will settle at the international level.

The 15-year phaseout of the Procampo income supports coincides with the 15-year transition to free trade in corn and beans agreed to in NAFTA. The two initiatives are clearly linked. Yet, Mexico would have found it necessary to alter its agricultural policy even without NAFTA. It could no longer afford to provide the resources to maintain the distortions inherent in the old policy.

The question raised by Procampo is whether it will in fact slow down the exodus from rural Mexico, thus dampening the short-term emigration effect into the United States. This will be hard to measure because so many other things will be taking place simultaneously. It may prove impossible to isolate the income-support measures from all other occurrences.

In the interim, before the hoped-for emigration-dampening effect of long-term economic growth takes hold, the United States is reacting to immigration pressures. The 1.3 million apprehensions of illegal immigrants in fiscal year 1993 was some 70 thousand higher than in fiscal year 1992 and about 130 thousand higher than in fiscal year 1991. The trend in apprehensions is upward, whether because there are more illegal entries or better border enforcement, or both, is unclear. The apprehension figures do not measure individuals because the same person may be apprehended, returned to Mexico, and then apprehended again many times during a year. Other illegal border crossers will not be apprehended. The INS in 1993 strengthened its border patrol at El Paso, Texas, leading to a sharp drop of illegal entries into that city. It is less clear, however, whether this reduced overall illegal entries or led merely to a shift of entries via other points of entry along the U.S.-Mexican border.

The U.S. Justice Department and the INS have asked for additional funds to augment the personnel and resources of the border patrol all along the Mexican border.

Both these actions, the El Paso blockade, as it was called for a while, and the proposal for increased surveillance all along the border, were taken without prior consultation with Mexico, but the two sides have since begun what one newspaper article called "more neighborly exchanges."[19]

Although not included in NAFTA, the subject of immigration is a salient element in the economic and social interaction of Mexico and the United States. It is one of the issues that makes economic relationships in North America different from those between the United States and other countries in the Americas with which free trade agreements are under discussion. The Mexico-U.S. relationship differs from all the others, and immigration and related labor issues are an important aspect of this difference.

Conclusion

This chapter stresses how much interaction occurs among the three countries of North America. U.S. business transactions – trade, investment, and other alliances – are greater with Canada than with any other country. U.S. people relations – matters of border crossing, kinship, illegal immigration – are greater with Mexico than with any other country. Given the lack of threat from either Mexico or Canada, these issues dropped from sight during the cold war. It is now time to put first things first; neighborhood, especially with a populous neighbor like Mexico, should take priority in U.S. thinking after the cold war.

4

The Meaning of Deepening

A nation's constitution can evolve into a more perfect union or serve as a subterfuge for repression. A charter like NAFTA, designed to encourage economic interchange between nations, can instead become a cover under which protectionism can exert its influence in more occult forms. The supposed economic integration agreements entered into in Latin America in the 1960s were really a technique to widen the area of protectionism for member countries; they were not movements toward trade liberalization. The use of integration agreements for protectionist purposes is not a new phenomenon; Jacob Viner discussed earlier examples in his classic book on economic integration, *The Customs Union Issue*, published in 1950.

It is in no way foreordained that NAFTA will become a truly liberalizing economic area in which the full benefits of free movement of goods, services, and capital will be permitted. It is not inevitable that production will be allowed to take place in the optimum location in North America based on relative factor costs, technical availability, access to markets, and the ability to move goods and services efficiently using modern communication and transportation facilities. Nor is there any guarantee that workers in the three countries will benefit from increased productivity, as market economics posits they should. It is uncertain how effectively the environment will be safeguarded.

NAFTA can become a model of *strong* integration under which the full range of these potential benefits will be obtained, or it can turn into just another example of *weak* integration whose purpose is largely to bestow preferences on member countries – or on producers in member countries – without regard to either the general welfare or the welfare of nonmember countries. In my view, a weak NAFTA will collapse of its own internal inconsistencies, as protective Latin American integration collapsed in less than a few decades in the 1960s and 1970s and other wider preferential areas, like Commonwealth preferences, died after longer periods. By contrast, I believe that a strong NAFTA can be more durable and generate its own momentum. This chapter examines some of the elements required for NAFTA to deepen into a strong form of economic integration.

NAFTA has much going for it.[1] It starts out with low border barriers so that tariff discrimination against nonmembers will not be formidable. The agreement is comprehensive and therefore deals with key elements for success. Resources are being invested to upgrade infrastructure. A nascent machinery is being put in place to monitor trade conflicts, customs procedures, and environmental protection. Domestic laws, at federal and state (or provincial) levels, are being changed to conform with the provisions of NAFTA.

But NAFTA also has much working against its development into a strong form of integration. New standards and regulations are being written that would protect local producers and favor them under government procurement. National laws dealing with alleged cases of dumping and subsidization of exports remain in effect and are growing in importance now that many other avenues of protection are foreclosed under the agreement. The rules of origin for free trade in key products – automotive, in particular, by far the most important sector in North American trade – are highly protectionist. The machinery of NAFTA, although more substantial than many of its critics contend, is still primitive. And just as NAFTA is in its formative stage, the nasty, unwanted issue of immigration is heating up. So, too, is nationalism, perhaps nowhere more intensely than in the United States.

There is much clamor from elsewhere in the Americas for accession to NAFTA. Although this is the theme for chapter 5, the issue is worth signaling here because it relates to the evolution of NAFTA as a form of strong integration as opposed to a wider preferential arrangement. At issue are the conditions to be imposed on countries wishing to accede to NAFTA—whether the terms will weaken the discipline achieved in the NAFTA negotiations or stringently insist that the price of entry is to conform to NAFTA disciplines as contained in the agreement and as they develop over time. Supporters of this or that country argue that political considerations require admission to NAFTA even if this diminishes the deepening in North America. Such reasoning must be resisted. As this chapter and the next argue, the first objective should be to deepen NAFTA lest its benefits be dissipated in the name of ephemeral political convenience.

Key Elements of Deepening

The first wave of economic integration after World War II—just as earlier waves under imperial preferences—emphasized reducing border barriers among member nations. One of the main expected benefits was the tariff preferences nations granted each other and the consequent effects of these to promote production in the member countries. The EEC's effort to achieve a customs union started this way, but always had a deepening objective. When EFTA was formed in response to the EEC, its main feature was to eliminate border barriers. The integration movements in Latin America were explicitly fashioned to broaden the scope for import substitution.

Once the initial steps were taken, however, it became clear that tariff and nontariff preferences did not constitute effective economic integration. Other forms of inefficiencies and protection became evident when the more visible impediments of border barriers were removed. The world learned this same lesson in successive rounds of GATT negotiations; after tariffs came down, other impediments loomed larger. The Contracting Parties to the GATT found it necessary in later negotiations to tackle what have come to be called "new" issues. Tariff reduction came first, then nontariff discipline, then trade in services, investment issues, intellectual property, and even the sacred cow of agriculture. The years ahead will require addressing other issues, such as the need to deal with the environmental effects of trade expansion and competition policy. The onionskin nature of economic integration has become apparent; another layer of restrictions almost always lurks below the one removed.

This verity was most clearly demonstrated in the EC, by far the most advanced of the economic integration movements. The main feature of Europe '92 was to eliminate market fragmentation to augment integration benefits. The costs of the remaining impediments to trade and production among the member countries – which were categorized under three major headings as physical, technical, and fiscal barriers – were popularized by Paolo Cecchini.[2] He quantified the costs for such barriers as incompatible and laborious customs procedures among member countries, divergent product standards, and rigged government procurement systems. The EC also searched for techniques to achieve tax harmonization, or at least neutralization, an issue not discussed here, but which will become important in North America if other aspects of deepening are achieved.[3]

Apart from this practical quantification of costs, it had become clear in the writings of economic theorists, like Nobel laureate R.H. Coase, that there is a world of "positive transaction costs."[4] Among other features, Coase had in mind studying legal systems and institutional structures for their effects on what happens from the time of the purchase of factors of production to the sale of the goods produced by these factors. In the case of U.S.-Mexico integration, Ewell Murphy has called attention to the importance of bridging the gap between the Mexican structure of judge-directed civil law and the U.S. version of jury-directed common law to obtain maximum benefit from NAFTA.[5] An ambitious project now exists that looks toward harmonizing trade and investment laws in Mexico and the United States.[6] Harmonization, or at least compatibility, of laws and regulations arises just as sharply in many other areas of NAFTA, such as customs procedures; sanitary and phytosanitary standards; interpretation of rules of origin; and product, trucking, and environmental standards.

Regulations and Standards

Industrial coproduction can be effective only if standards are either identical or compatible, depending on the product, in the producing countries. Standardization is a natural corollary of producing parts of final products in various locations for assembly in perhaps still another location. The color of the wires in an electrical system, or the size and configuration of the engine for a particular car model, or the wiring on a semiconductor for a computer, must be consistent no matter where produced under a structure of world production. Standards are usually not a major problem for intrafirm production in industries such as automotive parts production and computers, because companies can control these standards within their own extended firms.

Consistency becomes more complicated in intraindustry trade where many firms are involved. If parts producers send their product to many end users, control becomes increasingly complex. Still, such issues are still relatively simple because they can be managed with little interference from governments. Private associations of producers in the same industry in one country can work out the desired standards. But agreements are more elusive when they have to be worked out across national boundaries, as is the case in NAFTA, particularly if the original standards vary in the different societies.

Perhaps the most difficult area is when countries or private associations use standards not to facilitate coproduction and trade, but precisely to impede them. If tariff protection is not an option in an economic integration arrangement, then protectionism can take other forms – and there are as many ways to protect a national industry as there are people with vivid imaginations. Perhaps the most famous example of protectionism in the guise of standard setting emerged in the Cassis de Dijon decision of 1978 of the European Court of Justice. The court ruled that a German law requiring liqueurs to have a minimum alcohol content of 25 percent, thereby preventing the sale of the French liqueur Cassis de Dijon, could not be justified on health grounds and was thereby struck down.[7] An example of restrictive standards closer to home was the continuing effort of competing producers in the United States to limit the import of vine-ripened tomatoes from Mexico; one example of this effort was the drafting of a marketing order by the U.S. Department of Agriculture specifying that tomatoes shipped in the same crate must be of uniform size. This is relatively simple to do for tomatoes that are picked green and then chemically ripened, but much harder when tomatoes ripen naturally, on the vine from the sun.[8]

New examples of using standards and regulations for protective purposes are emerging even now in U.S.-Mexico trade. On March 7, 1994, Mexico enforced a standard already in place, but not previously implemented, that required computers entering the country to be labeled in Spanish without the use of sticky labels. The decision, which went into effect overnight, caused many sales to be canceled. Although the new standard had been published in the official Mexican gazette, similar earlier notices had not always been enforced. In addition, Mexico, using Harmonized System tariff identifiers, specified that home computers and household appliances entering the country must be certified by a specified list of Mexican companies, some of these actual competitors of the exporting companies. In addition, a Mexican official announced in a speech that Mexico will issue 600 new standards in 1994, but their content was not made clear, nor did he say how much notice will be given.

There may not be a protective intent in these examples, but rather a desire on the part of Mexico to establish its own standards regime in anticipation of the time that NAFTA calls for mutual certification. Yet the process surely impedes trade, the very opposite of what NAFTA is intended to accomplish. It is hard to erase a long-established bureaucratic culture in Mexico under which every detail of import transactions is controlled—from license approval to basing the amount of import duty to be paid on an artificially determined value of a product, one always higher than the invoice price. This culture must change if NAFTA is to succeed.

Nor does the United States escape blame in violating the spirit of NAFTA and diluting the benefits Mexico hoped to achieve from integration. To promote U.S. grain sales to Mexico in competition with allegedly subsidized wheat exports from Canada, the United States began to provide its own subsidies under the Export Enhancement Program. These export subsidies make it exceedingly difficult for Mexican authorities to carry out their own agricultural program of eventually allowing agricultural product prices to be determined by supply and demand forces in the international market. Mexico is thus caught in an export-subsidy war between the United States and Canada—a far cry from free trade. The United States and Canada both profess belief in free trade, except when domestic politics calls for subsidized exports, particularly for agricultural products.

Mexican avocados are denied entry into the United States on the ground that they are diseased and could contaminate the California crop. Fumigation requirements hamper the entry of U.S. fruits into Mexico. There are suspicions that the true motive on both sides is protectionism.

The purpose of entering into an economic integration agreement as opposed to putting exclusive reliance on the multilateral structure of the GATT is that regionalism permits greater progress in harmonizing practices that affect production and trade. None of these potential areas of harmonization is more important than setting product standards and refraining from using regulatory powers to replace older and more transparent — at least to the general public, if not to the producers and traders caught up in the web of protection — methods of favoring domestic economic interests. The potential for the discriminatory use of standards is immense, indeed infinite for practical purposes. If even a small part of this potential is exploited, NAFTA can prove to be a mug's game of action and reaction, of protection and retaliation.

What can be done other than exhortation? On the regulatory front, a system is needed under which each of the member countries of NAFTA and their private producers are able to penetrate the processes of the other two countries. This system has to be institutionalized, just as it is within countries. The hearings on new or altered regulations require advance publicity and transparency. Failing these measures, NAFTA will surely be diminished.

These are not revolutionary suggestions. In fact, they are contemplated in various articles of the agreement dealing with notification, publication, and the provision of information (article 909), establishment of a committee on standards-related measures (article 913, which calls for the committee to meet at least once a year and at the request of any member country), and the ability to consult on the operation of NAFTA (article 2006).[9] The supplemental agreements on environmental and labor cooperation provide other examples of penetrating the regulatory and standard-setting processes of the member countries in these fields.

Institutionalizing this type of penetration into what is generally considered to be a domestic prerogative—that is, the writing of national regulations—entails some derogation of sovereignty. But the sacrifice is minimal and is in the interest of effecting an agreement all three countries entered into freely. What is involved is for each country to prevent the dilution of benefits it thought it had obtained from the agreement. Most standards are prepared not by governments, but private interest groups, at least in the United States. Business groupings—textile producers, automakers, chemical manufacturers, computer organizations, et cetera—and associations of engineers, doctors, accountants, lawyers, and other professionals are all engaged in setting standards. These, too, must be monitored by the private groups of the other member countries. If NAFTA is to work optimally, these associations will have to become trinational in their composition, at least for the purpose of setting standards.

I have dwelled on this issue precisely because it is complex and raises sensitive issues within each of the three NAFTA countries. But I have emphasized it as well because it goes to the very heart of making NAFTA an effective form of economic integration.

The Institutionalization of NAFTA

NAFTA, in contrast to the EU, was designed to minimize the creation of new institutions. The designers succeeded, in the sense that there is no overarching commission with an expert secretariat able to analyze issues, call attention to shortcomings of member countries in complying with obligations of the underlying treaty, or make proposals about new initiatives. There is no such thing as a NAFTA directive that becomes the law of the three countries, as in the EU. NAFTA does not have the kinds of political institutions that were created when the EEC was established, such as a parliament or its own court of justice to rule on complaints under the agreement.

Yet these differences do not mean that NAFTA has no institutions. Indeed, the array of commissions, committees, working groups, panels, ad hoc advisory bodies, and other technical arrangements is mind boggling. Only a partial listing will be given here. The Free Trade Commission is the cabinet-level body charged with supervising the implementation of the agreement. It can establish ad hoc or standing committees and working or expert groups. This commission is required to meet only once a year. Although not formally part of NAFTA itself, the two supplemental agreements establish their own commissions, one on environmental cooperation and the other on labor cooperation. Each of these has its own structure, with its own subbodies. The site of the three commissions was deliberately spread across the three member countries – the free trade commission in Mexico City, the environmental commission in Montreal, and the labor commission in Dallas. A North American Development Bank (NADBank) was created to raise funds by borrowing from private markets for infrastructure at or near the U.S.-Mexico border; its home is to be in San Antonio.

The agreement itself establishes committees on trade in goods, worn clothing, and agriculture; there are committees on sanitary and phytosanitary measures, standards, small business, financial services, and finally an advisory committee on private commercial disputes. The committee on standards-related measures has subcommittees on land transportation, telecommunications, automotive matters, and labeling of textiles and apparel. There are working groups on customs procedures, rules of origin, agricultural subsidies, trade and competition, and temporary entry of persons.

Beyond these, NAFTA calls for the establishment of rosters of arbitral panels on disputes arising out of dumping and countervailing duties (chapter 19) and other trade disputes (chapter 20). Although there is no court of justice, chapter 19 does establish procedures under which a panel can review final dumping or countervailing duty determinations of the competent authorities of the importing country. These arbitration findings are binding, except for the right of review by an extraordinary challenge committee.

NAFTA thus has the machinery to facilitate the deepening of integration among the three countries if they desire. This machinery is unlikely to be adequate if NAFTA were broadened to many other countries; that would require a more substantial secretariat with more staff and greater powers to facilitate consultation among a greater number of members. Such an enlargement of power of a central commission would not be easily accepted by the United States, and perhaps not by the other two members either, out of abhorrence of creating additional international institutions.[10]

The institutional structure of NAFTA was dictated not only by concern over excessive bureaucracy, but by the fact that North America has one country with overwhelming economic and political power and two less powerful neighbors. The situation is quite different from Europe, where the economic dominance of Germany is less thoroughgoing and where the structure was designed to harness Germany's preponderance. Canada, when it proposed integration with the United States, deliberately chose the FTA option rather than a customs union precisely to avoid a common external tariff or a common commercial policy that it feared would be dictated by the United States. The FTA format, according to Canadian economist Richard Lipsey, reduces the U.S. penchant to use trade policy for foreign policy and is therefore less likely than a customs union to become inward looking.[11] Canada obviously did not want to be dragged along in the U.S. use of foreign economic coercion, such as the economic embargo of Cuba. Mexico felt the same way, and undoubtedly the United States also wished more freedom to act than it would have if there were a customs union and a common commercial policy. Structure was dictated, therefore, by politics and power asymmetry as much as by economics.

Yet the effectiveness and durability of NAFTA will depend on making use of the machinery that exists, then embedding North American, as opposed to national, habits of thinking into the practice of using the institutions that are created. Some examples make this point:

- Customs delays at the border will have to shortened if a just-in-time inventory policy is to be followed.
- The United States must resolve migration concerns by some means other than a blockade on border crossing if it really seeks the benefits of coproduction with Mexico.
- Mexico must refrain from last-minute changes in standards for the entry of U.S. goods if it aspires to facilitate cross-border trade and investment.
- The United States must refrain from asking Mexico to open its market for U.S. grains and then subsidizing these exports into Mexico.
- Mexico will have to make changes in its civil law – a minefield that permits long terms of imprisonment for alleged fraud – if trade and investment are to be facilitated.
- The United States will have to learn the good grace to accept those decisions it may lose in arbitration cases under chapter 19 dealing with subsidies and countervailing duties – as has happened repeatedly in disputes with Canada.

As investment and trade in goods and services grow among the NAFTA countries, private actors will inevitably seek less volatility in exchange rates. So, too, will the three governments. Wide swings in exchange rates can substantially affect trade and capital flows, as has been evident in North America in recent years. This position in favor of greater exchange-rate stability was made explicit in April 1994 when the three NAFTA central banks opened a "trilateral foreign-exchange swap facility" to "maintain orderly exchange markets."[12] The swap line to Mexico is $6 billion from the United States and $800 million from Canada, plus a $2 billion swap line from the United States to Canada. It is most unlikely that a line-of-credit, which is what a central bank swap is, of this magnitude would have been considered by the United States if NAFTA were not in existence.

Some respected economists go so far as to advocate eventual monetary union, but this is not a widely held view.[13] This form of institutionalization, which goes well beyond what the three countries contemplate, would entail greater sacrifice of sovereignty – a loss of monetary policy independence – for Mexico and Canada than they had bargained for when they chose the FTA format. The opposite argument is that these two countries have limited scope even now for independent monetary policy because of their great financial and trade dependence on the United States; but having limited scope is different from having no scope. There are also major technical problems in a currency union, particularly if there are major differences in inflation and fiscal discipline.

When Canada in the first instance, and then Mexico subsequently, proposed entering into FTAs with the United States, one of the motives was defensive – to insulate their exports from what they feared was growing U.S. protectionism. Increasingly, U.S. competitors were resorting to contingent protection – that is, charging exporters in other countries with dumping their goods in the U.S. market or obtaining subsidies from their governments. Dumping is selling goods at less than fair value, but this term of art has taken on a complex meaning in U.S. trade law and policy. At any rate, charges of dumping became the protective device of choice in the United States and is being emulated elsewhere around the world.

The Canadians argued that dumping was an inappropriate concept for use in a free trade area. The Mexicans later argued the same. The logic was that if a product is sold within the United States, say, from Detroit to Chicago, discriminatory pricing – that is, selling for less in

Chicago than in some other location in the United States—was permissible, unless a predatory motive could be demonstrated. In the latter case, restrictive business safeguards could be used. If the same product was sold from Windsor, Ontario, just across the border from Detroit, to Chicago under exactly the same conditions, antidumping laws applied. This, the Canadians argued, was less than free trade.

The Canadians failed in their effort, as did the Mexicans. Article 1902 of NAFTA is quite explicit: "Each Party reserves the right to apply its antidumping law and countervailing duty law to goods imported from the territory of any other Party." Canada and Mexico thus failed to get protection against the use of these so-called fair-trade laws—they failed, that is, to accomplish one of their major objectives in the negotiation.

The compromise worked out first in the Canadian FTA and then, in modified form, in NAFTA, was the right of review of antidumping and countervailing duty matters (AD and CVD), embodied in chapter 19. This permitted a complaining country to replace judicial review of AD and CVD decisions with a binational panel review to determine if an AD or CVD determination accorded with the imposing country's own law. A provision in the Canada-U.S. FTA called for a review of this whole matter over a five-year period, which could be extended to seven years. This provision was dropped in NAFTA. At the end of 1993, however, when the Liberals took over the Canadian government, the United States agreed to review the AD and CVD issue at the insistence of Prime Minister Jean Chrétien. There the matter now stands.

Because AD and CVD issues are important in U.S. trade practice, they have been much analyzed. Of the two, the AD controversy has been more intense. It is possible, in theory at least, to replace national AD laws with competition law in a free trade area, but it is harder to get at subsidy issues without actually reviewing how subsidies are used within each country. Canada subsidizes many ac-

TABLE 4-1
U.S. Antidumping and Countervailing
Duty Activity, 1991–1993
(number of cases)

	1991	1992	1993 (Jan.–Oct.)
Antidumping duties			
Investigations	66	84	23
Duty imposed	19	17	62
Duty revocations	7	2	3
Countervailing duties			
Investigations	10	22	2
Duty imposed	2	4	16
Duty revocations	6	0	2

Source: GATT, *Trade Policy Review Mechanism: United States*, report by the U.S. government, C/RM/45, January 19, 1994, p. 36.

tivities; so, in fact, do the other two countries—for example, when a U.S. state or locality provides tax abatements and other benefits to attract investors.

Table 4-1 shows the recent evolution of U.S. AD and CVD activity. The significant figures here are the number of duties imposed in 1993, especially AD duties. The duty is imposed only after a double finding—that dumping took place and that a domestic industry was injured.

The binational panel process for reviewing AD determinations has proved to be more effective than originally anticipated, at least for Canada. In case after case, the panels have concluded that the U.S. AD margin (or CVD margin in subsidy cases) has been larger than warranted by the evidence presented, or even that a penalty duty was warranted. Indeed, the United States has lost so many high-profile cases, in whole or in part (involving softwood lumber, red raspberries, pork, and live swine, among other products) that there has been a political clamor in the U.S.

Congress that the process is stacked against the United States, or that the panelists have exceeded their authority. There also has been a tendency for AD and CVD cases to return endlessly in modified form. This is especially true for softwood lumber imports into the United States from Canada. Politics often dominates the arbitral process.

This volume is not the place to review all the elements of AD practice, except to highlight that the issue has become contentious on a global basis and, in the context of this discussion, in North American relations.[14] The general consensus is that U.S. law and practice in this field is itself unfair, or more colorfully, that the laws in both Canada and the United States are "wacko."[15] The major concern with the U.S. law is that it invites AD petitions and the initiation of such a case has the effect of impeding trade regardless of the ultimate finding. The concern with the administration of U.S. law is that it is arbitrary and stacked against the exporter.

Many critics seek a solution in eliminating national AD laws in the context of NAFTA and replacing these with competition policy. This position is taken by Thomas Boddez and Michael Trebilcock (see note 14). This goal would be difficult to achieve unless the integration of the three countries becomes much more comprehensive than is contemplated; it would require changes in all three national laws and possibly the establishment of some supranational competition regime. Other proposals deal more modestly with the details of U.S. practice. This is the position of most contributors to a volume edited by Richard Boltuck and Robert E. Litan (see note 14). In any event, as the title of the Boddez-Trebilcock book indicates, this is a piece of "unfinished business" in NAFTA.

Finally, still under the rubric of institutionalization of NAFTA, deepening requires some technique for more effective consultation among the three countries on a broad range of issues. The central banks were able to act rapidly to set up the swap line to defend the value of the peso when the assassination of Luis Donaldo Colosio roiled financial markets in Mexico because they had been consulting on just this theme during 1993. Mexico reacted with annoyance when the El Paso immigration blockade was introduced, in part because the Mexican authorities were not informed or consulted in advance. As a result, immigration consultations are now taking place. U.S. computer exporters were annoyed, in turn, when Mexico changed import labeling laws over a single night. The United States has requested more consultation before new regulations and standards are promulgated and implemented. And Mexican authorities have visited the U.S. Department of Agriculture to plead for some understanding of the cost to the Mexican program of U.S. and Canadian competitive grain export subsidies.

It will take time for the practices of consultation to become embedded in North America. The word "consultation," not "coordination," is used advisedly. It is hard, perhaps impossible, to coordinate macroeconomic policy when economic integration does not contemplate economic and monetary union, as in the EU. Yet U.S. macroeconomic policy actions have a major impact on Mexico. When U.S. interest rates were raised sharply in the early 1980s, this may have affected Mexico even more than the United States because of Mexico's high external debt. As the U.S. Federal Reserve raised interest rates in 1984, this too has a profound impact on Mexico's economy. As U.S. long-term interest rates rise, Mexico is constrained in the extent to which it can use expansionary monetary policy to stimulate its economy at a time of low growth. The level of U.S. interest rates also influences the choice of where portfolio investment is made, in Mexican or U.S. bonds.

Consultation with Mexico is much more extensive than it has been in the past. But the task of NAFTA is to make this routine, to institutionalize it at all levels and not just at cabinet-level meetings that last a day or two each year. The consultation can help work out problems dealing with new regulations and standards; it can prevent petty annoyances from occurring; and it can be used to forewarn counterparts about what is contemplated even if each country, in the final analysis, must decide for itself what is in its national interest.

Nongovernmental Cooperation

Although NAFTA is an intergovernmental agreement, its effectiveness depends on cooperation among private groups. Devising North American product, trucking, and environmental standards requires the input of business associations and nongovernmental organizations or NGOs. Organized labor in the United States failed in its effort to defeat NAFTA, but there is nevertheless growing cooperation between labor unions in Mexico and the United States.

As Cathryn Thorup has pointed out, positions on issues are not necessarily defined solely within the country from which a private businessperson or an NGO comes, but frequently by cross-country coalitions.[16] A U.S. corporation producing goods in Mexico through an affiliate or a strategic partner may have more in common with allied producers in Mexico than with competing U.S. producers and exporters. A coalition to unionize Mexican factories may pit labor union leaders in the two countries against producers in the two countries. Environmentalists may make common cause, no matter where located. And human rights advocates will make more progress if they cooperate across national lines rather than confine themselves to a single country.

The development of the environmental provisions of NAFTA is instructive of the kinds of coalitions that are likely to develop in the future. When environmentalists in the United States first proposed the inclusion of these issues in the NAFTA agreement, the first reaction of the U.S. and Mexican governments was opposition. Many business interests were opposed to the inclusion of these issues out of fear that this would dilute the trade and investment primacy of the agreement. The Mexican environmental movement played a small role at first, primarily because it was still in the formative stage. This role grew as the debate continued and Mexican environmentalists gained both strength and confidence. The inclusion of environmental issues in both the body of the agreement and in the supplemental understandings now gives a much more important role to the Mexican movement. A coalition that barely existed before NAFTA is now in place and can only intensify over time.

The future will bring many more cross-border alliances. Governments will disagree and there will be cross-border conflicts, but there must also be cooperation among nongovernmental actors transcending national lines. NAFTA cannot deepen unless this takes place.

The Cultural Dimension

When a Mexican refers to a national of the United States, he (she) refers to him (her) as a *norteamericano* (or *norteamericana*). But North America is defined in NAFTA as including Mexico. We will know that NAFTA has entered into the popular culture of Mexico when Mexicans also refer to themselves as *norteamericanos*. They will then have to find another word for people from the United States.[17]

Familiarization of each culture with the other is a more substantial manifestation of deepening than the growth of cross-border alliances. The latter normally take place because of a specific interest — the environment, unionization, coproduction. These issues are important; indeed, they are at the heart of economic and social cooperation in North America. But when the peoples of the three countries understand more profoundly the forces that shape the others, deepening occurs for its own sake. This kind of deepening will make for permanent coalitions, instead of the shifting alliances that are more likely to occur on economic issues.

The people of the United States know little of Mexican

history. And it was obvious during the debate on NAFTA that the interest groups and politicians also knew little. The debate was based on stereotypes: Mexicans are corrupt; they have no social consciousness; the country is non-democratic; the president is a dictator for six years; human rights are completely disregarded there; and Mexicans cannot be expected to pay much heed to their environment unless prodded by U.S. sanctions of one kind or another. Much of the anti-immigrant fervor assumed that all—or most—Mexicans would flee to the United States if given half an opportunity.

There was little knowledge demonstrated about how Mexico arrived at the political system it has. There was little recognition of the sense of pride that Mexicans have in their culture, one much older than the cultures of the other two countries of NAFTA. The influence of the revolution of 1910 and the subsequent civil war on Mexican patterns of thinking were never explored. The debate, put simply, was most demeaning to Mexicans—hardly a propitious way to start a relationship that must deepen if it is to endure.

Mexicans know a little more about what shapes actions across the border if only because news of the United States is a daily feature in the Mexican media. Millions of Mexicans have lived in the United States. But the knowledge is superficial. It goes something like this: Americans seek domination, act without principle if that suits their purpose, and can be rapacious, as is evident from the history of relations between the two countries. It is almost as though the period of U.S. manifest destiny is still with us.

But the NAFTA debate was a step toward cultural understanding. NAFTA has also stimulated thought about an idea of forging a educational common market—more sojourns by students and professors traveling in both directions, and greater attention in school curricula, at all levels, of the history and culture of the other two countries. Before NAFTA, there were practically no university programs in Mexico dedicated to the study of the United

States, let alone Canada; there are many now. NAFTA stimulated a rush to affiliations between universities in the three countries. Mexican cultural exhibits are now frequent in the United States, including the blockbuster show, "Mexico: Splendors of 30 Centuries."

The issue needs no belaboring. NAFTA, if it is to meet its objectives, must be more than a business arrangement. Although this goal was not part of the original idea, the need for it is now evident.

Sovereignty

NAFTA poses a modest dilemma. It will not endure unless it deepens in the ways discussed here; but deepening, if it happens, will require some diminution of national sovereignty. The word "modest" is intended to stress that the sovereignty issues are overstated. They are used to distort and defeat, not clarify, the real issues.

Mexico and Canada, the two smaller countries, might have been expected to have the greatest concerns about dilution of sovereignty. An election was fought in Canada in 1988 about whether the FTA with the United States went too far in pushing Canada into the economic orbit of the United States. In the end, the Conservative Party won that election, and the FTA went into effect. In Mexico, when Salinas was campaigning for president, he made a speech on foreign policy in which he used some variant of the word "sovereign" at least 25 times.[18] After all, Mexicans have been raised on an emotional diet of noninterference in the internal affairs of other countries, a hangover from the loss of territory to the United States in the Treaty of Guadalupe Hidalgo of 1848 that ended the Mexican war. Yet, the biggest fuss about sovereignty was made in the United States.

Issues of sovereignty were raised in a number of contexts and complaints came from both the left and the right. The left contended that disputes would be settled in secret by arbitral panels, just as, it was alleged, the agreement itself was negotiated in secret. An anti-NAFTA ad in the *Washington Post* asserted that the agreement nullifies the "democratic" process.[19] The right raised the specter of immigration and how NAFTA would contribute to U.S. loss of control over its border. U.S. politician Pat Buchanan, under the theme of "putting America first," argued that NAFTA is "about a loss of American sovereignty."[20] Both extremes argued that the two supplemental agreements would involve the monitoring of U.S. laws by supranational commissions that could then impose fines and trade penalties for infractions.

The environmental agreement was analyzed with great care by a scholar from the Cato Institute, whose expected bias, given the libertarian creed of that think tank, would be to find a loss of sovereignty from the grant of monitoring and fining power to an international body. Jerry Taylor wrote: "Although the treaty encourages high environmental standards and the harmonization of environmental statutes, the sovereign right of nations to set their own levels of environmental protection is repeatedly and explicitly reaffirmed in the treaty."[21] Mickey Kantor, the U.S. Trade Representative, made the same point about the right of the United States under both supplemental agreements to write its own laws and set its own standards: "U.S. sovereignty is fully protected in these agreements. We insisted that no supranational body could usurp the right of each country to set its own laws, nor could such a body enforce our laws in place of federal, state, or local authorities."[22]

Yet, there is some diminution of sovereignty in that the two supplemental agreements give the trinational commissions the right to monitor enforcement of the internal laws of each of the three countries and to impose penalties in the event of nonenforcement as determined by an arbitration panel set up for this purpose. The penalties are not substantial, and the procedure to get to that point is deliberately cumbersome, but the commissions do have the authority to publicize their findings. A country is under no obligation to carry out the findings of a panel, but in that event the complaining country can withdraw benefits (that is, impose its own import restrictions) of an equivalent amount. These two agreements were directed at Mexico, but, like NAFTA itself, they are reciprocal.

The loss of sovereignty within NAFTA is no more drastic than that of many other international agreements. The United States, like the other two countries, agrees to abide by a series of commitments – tariff reductions, elimination of nontariff barriers, national treatment to foreign investors, among others – but these are comparable to obligations undertaken in other agreements, such as the GATT. The willingness to submit its AD and CVD decisions to panel review goes beyond obligations in other agreements, but this process has its safeguards in the presence of U.S. nationals on the panels and the right of extraordinary challenge.

The way two authors put it for a Mexican audience is that the definition of sovereignty must change as times change. In previous times, business sovereignty was defined by what was in the interest of leading national business figures (*cúpulas empresariales*), but this practice requires adaptation in times of globalization of production.[23] This is a reasonable formulation for the United States as well, the country most engaged in global production and trade.

Deepening as described here requires one further degree of derogation of sovereignty – countries will have to find some way to expose their new regulations and product standards to the other member countries as a precaution against using these techniques to dilute the benefits expected from NAFTA. Legislators will have to be alert not to pass laws that have the same effect. These conditions are not onerous, especially when undertaken reciprocally. It can be argued that sovereignty under this kind of deepening is not diminished by NAFTA, but enlarged in that each member country is able to penetrate the processes of the others to safeguard its national interest.

Conclusion

The message of this chapter is that NAFTA must deepen if it is to survive. The requirement for much of this deepening is written right into the agreement in the form of permanent committees and working groups established for this purpose. This deepening will take place quietly as government officials negotiate technical details of customs procedures, rules of origin, sanitary standards, and monetary policy issues with each other. Except when a multibillion dollar swap line is opened, the results of these discussions will not be spectacular. The purpose is to fill in the operating procedures of NAFTA. There could be no NAFTA without these.

But deepening must go beyond the work of government officials. It is the private sector that has most at stake. Product standards affect them primarily. NGOs must form cross-border coalitions to carry out their assigned tasks. Once again, NAFTA would be meaningless without these activities.

But deepening must go beyond even that. There must be some way to penetrate the regulation-writing processes of the three national governments and their subunits to prevent dilution of expected benefits in this guise. And some unfinished business remains – how to reduce the bitterness that is being engendered by the profligate use of contingent protection in the form of AD and CVD measures.

Finally, deepening will have been successful when these activities directly related to NAFTA are expanded into closer cultural understanding of each other in North America. NAFTA, in other words, should become more than a business deal.

5

The Widening of NAFTA

President George Bush set forth his vision of free trade from Alaska to Tierra del Fuego in his Enterprise for the Americas Initiative (EAI) of June 1990. The idea was received enthusiastically in most of Latin America and the Caribbean (LAC).[1] There were a number of reasons for this welcome:

- The proposal addressed a critical issue in the hemisphere's development aspirations – easier and more assured access to the U.S. market for the region's exports.
- Most of the countries were reducing their import barriers unilaterally, and the further gradual reduction implied in an FTA was no longer unthinkable.
- And massive foreign aid – a new Marshall Plan or Alliance for Progress for the region – was not a viable option.

As of mid-1994, four years later, nothing much had happened to implement the initiative. The Clinton administration went through an ordeal to obtain congressional approval of NAFTA at the end of 1993 and had little stomach for repeating this process too quickly. On their part, many LAC countries had second thoughts. They wanted reasonably assured access to the U.S. market, but were concerned that the price that had to be paid for accession to NAFTA might be a bit rich for them. What has been called restructuring fatigue emerged in a number of countries. Venezuela and Costa Rica, which earlier had considered themselves to be prime candidates to join NAFTA, elected new presidents who, in essence, said they wished to reconsider the reforms under way in their own countries.

Reaching a Western Hemisphere Free Trade Association will be a laborious and time-consuming process; indeed, it may never be reached. Yet, it remains an objective in most of the hemisphere, a limit to be aimed at even if not fully achieved. Some LAC countries may not want free trade with or within NAFTA, at least not yet.[2] So be it. But it remains clear that most LAC countries want some trade understandings with the United States. The free trade proposal of the EAI, assuming it still is operative, may not be taken up by everybody in the hemisphere, but there would be a general accusation of bad faith were the offer removed from the table.

We are witnessing a process of hemispheric introspection. Yes, we want some assurance of an open U.S. market, but we are not sure of the price we wish to pay. Yes, we wish to hold open the prospect of hemispheric free trade, but we do not know when. We do not know how long it will take to get to a WHFTA, but there must be some interim measures. We know that accession to NAFTA is one way to get to hemispheric free trade, but there must be other techniques. Some of these issues are on the agenda of the hemispheric summit of December 1994 in Miami—but almost certainly will not be resolved there.[3]

The main part of this chapter—following some background material on the integration scene in the hemisphere and the stakes for the parties in further integration—is a discussion of how to get from here to there; how to get from what exists to a WHFTA or whatever emerges in freeing inter-American trade. The suggestions made are guided by the following principles:

1. An expansion of NAFTA to new countries should not prejudice the deepening of economic relations in North America. This principle defines the entry price: The enter-

ing country must commit itself to the undertakings in NAFTA. A reasonable transition period with minor derogations can be the subject of the accession negotiation.

2. Because not all countries will be able to or interested in acceding to NAFTA under these conditions, other arrangements short of full accession should be considered so as not to prejudice the trade and investment interests of these countries.

3. Accession should be to NAFTA and not to a series of bilateral agreements by individual NAFTA members with countries outside the agreement.[4]

4. It is in the interest of hemispheric development to strengthen the subregional integration movements that exist outside of North America.[5] For this reason, it would be preferable for NAFTA, as a unit, to work out free trade arrangements with other subregional groupings rather than with individual countries of these groupings.

5. Finally, open regionalism not only requires low border barriers, but also a commitment by the various subregional groupings—including NAFTA—to keep open the possibility of accession by new countries under appropriate conditions.

The Integration Scene in the Americas

Free trade between the United States and LAC countries as proposed in the EAI grows out of a shift in U.S. policy toward bilateralism and regionalism. This shift can be explained by the growth of regionalism in Europe, the emergence of persistent U.S. trade deficits and the consequent willingness to try new models of trade policy, and frustration with the workings of GATT.[6] It is now conventional, even if not unanimous, wisdom that regionalism and globalism in trade can be pursued simultaneously. I would argue somewhat differently—that regionalism is here to stay, at least for the indefinite future, so it is essential to make it compatible with globalism.

U.S. economic regionalism found its main outlet for more than a century in establishing a large national market. Cross-country regionalism has a longer history in Latin America, going back to the Bolivarian dream of political integration and then emerging again, this time in its economic manifestation, after World War II as a way to widen the scope for import substitution. What is new for the LAC countries today is the acceptance of regional trade and economic arrangements with the United States. This is not the first time the United States has made a proposal for Western Hemisphere free trade, but it is the first time such an initiative has been taken seriously.[7] The main reason for the change is the transformation in development policy from looking inward to seeking extraregional markets for LAC exports; and what better market than the United States, the region's largest export destination? This dominance in the exports of Canada and Mexico helps explain why these two countries were the first to seek FTAs with the United States.

The tragic decade of the 1980s for the LAC countries was the stimulus for substantial changes in economic policy—from closed to more open economies, from state-dominated planning to greater scope for private enterprise, and from what one commentator called "defensive nationalism," which consisted of a combination of state domination and protected industries, to greater reliance on markets.[8]

The intensity of the shift from ultra-protectionism to open markets has not been uniform among all LAC countries, but the articulation of the new philosophy of greater import openness and export promotion has been nearly ubiquitous. Most Latin American countries now have tariffs that average below 20 percent, compared with levels as much as five times greater a decade ago. In the case of Mexico, the trade-weighted average tariff is about 11 percent. These tariff levels are still higher than those of the industrial countries, but they are no longer intended to generally exclude imports. Their further reduction over an extended transition period would not be traumatic. Nontariff barriers, such as prior import licensing, have also been dramatically reduced. These changes, taken unilaterally by the LAC countries, made possible the free trade initiative by Mexico, Chile's request for free trade negotiations with the United States, and the contemplation of hemispheric free trade on the part of LAC countries generally. They highlight an important point: Contemplation of free trade must come *after* much internal restructuring has occurred if the transition to free trade is to be accomplished in a reasonable number of years once an agreement is concluded.

In addition, this shift in mentality from protectionism, from safeguarding generally small markets and small production runs to playing a larger role on the world economic scene, has served to reinvigorate the regional integration arrangements among LAC countries. This activity can be seen in table 5-1, which lists only the main integration arrangements. The integration arrangements in the Western Hemisphere are a crazy-quilt pattern of cross memberships and nests of small integration arrangements within larger ones. The membership of the Andean Common Market or ANCOM overlaps that of the Latin American Integration Association (ALADI). So does the membership of the Southern Cone Common Market (MERCOSUR) overlap ALADI's. Mexico is a member of NAFTA and ALADI; has free trade agreements with Chile, Costa Rica, Colombia and Venezuela; and is engaged in integration talks with the Central American Economic Community (CACM). Colombia has approached the United States about possible free trade talks even as it retains membership in ALADI and ANCOM and is part of the Group of 3 free trade area with Mexico and Venezuela.

This proliferation of economic integration schemes and the multiple membership phenomenon will have to be sorted out one day. Each arrangement has its own rules, and the rules are not always consistent with each other. This complex structure will presumably give way to something more coherent if the process of hemispheric free trade ad-

TABLE 5-1
Main Integration Movements in the Americas

Movement	Year Established	Objective
ALADI	1980	Ultimate Latin American common market
ANCOM	1969	Common external tariff of 5 percent to 20 percent
Colombia-Venezuela	1991	Free trade
MERCOSUR	1991	CET by 1995
CACM	1960	Free trade and common trade policy
CARICOM	1973	Common market
Mexico-Chile	1991	Remove all tariffs and many NTBs
Costa Rica–Mexico	1994	Roughly same as Mexico-Chile
U.S.-Canada FTA	1989	Free trade, overtaken by NAFTA
NAFTA	1994	10 to 15 year transition to free trade

Source: Council of the Americas, *Washington Report*, winter 1992; and Moisés Naim, see note 2, this chapter.

Memberships:

ALADI (Latin American Integration Association): Argentina, Bolivia, Brazil, Colombia, Chile, Ecuador, Mexico, Paraguay, Peru, Uruguay, and Venezuela

ANCOM (Andean Common Market): Bolivia, Colombia, Ecuador, Peru, and Venezuela

MERCOSUR (Southern Cone Common Market): Argentina, Brazil, Paraguay, and Uruguay

CACM (Central American Economic Community): Costa Rica, El Salvador, Guatemala, Honduras, and Nicaragua

CARICOM (Caribbean Community): Antigua and Barbuda, Bahamas, Barbados, Belize, Dominica, Grenada, Guyana, Jamaica, Montserrat, St. Kitts and Nevis, St. Lucia, St. Vincent and the Grenadines, and Trinidad and Tobago

NAFTA (North American Free Trade Area): Canada, Mexico, and the United States vances further. I return to this theme when discussing sequencing of free trade and possible institutional arrangements as the process plays itself out.

For many years, intra-LAC trade languished. In 1982, for example, LAC exports to one another were only 14 percent of total exports, compared with 40 percent to the United States. In 1992, the proportion of intra-LAC exports grew to 18 percent, still modest when compared with the 42 percent to the United States, but it is on a growth path.[9] Trade among the countries of the subregional groupings, other than NAFTA, has also been growing, but is still quite modest — 20 percent of total exports for CACM, 14 percent of total exports for MERCOSUR, but less than 6 percent for CARICOM, and less than 5 percent for Colombia-Venezuela, all in 1992.[10]

The Stakes in Hemispheric Free Trade

This section looks first at the U.S. interest — to ask what prompted the Bush initiative for hemispheric free trade. It then examines the stakes for the other players — Canada and the LAC countries.

The U.S. Interest

Although Western Hemisphere countries took 38 percent of worldwide U.S. merchandise exports in 1993, about 80 percent of these were to the other two North American countries (see table 3-2). The static picture, therefore, does not demonstrate that the United States should have a great interest in expanding NAFTA to the rest of the Western Hemisphere. If anything, a snapshot of U.S. exports in 1993 would imply that the U.S. free trade interest, after North America, should focus on Asia and the Pacific, which was the destination of 28 percent of U.S. exports (see table 3-1).

Yet there is a dynamic picture that is more edifying. Between 1990 and 1992, U.S. exports worldwide grew, in current dollars, at an average annual rate of less than 7 percent. Those to countries in the Western Hemisphere other than Canada and Mexico, with which a free trade agreement already exists, grew at an average annual rate of 17 percent.[11] This was more substantial than U.S. export growth to Asian and Pacific countries or Western Europe, the two other important export destinations. The United States captures a larger share of LAC imports than it does of imports of other regions; consequently, the United States has a large commercial stake in economic growth in the Western Hemisphere.

The importance of this growth can be seen in a few statistics on the relationship between LAC economic performance and U.S. merchandise exports to the region. U.S. exports to LAC countries grew fivefold during the 1970s when the region's GDP grew at an annual rate of about 4.5 percent. By contrast, U.S. exports to the region grew by less than 50 percent during the 1980s, when GDP growth averaged only 1.5 percent a year. The trade figures are for exports in current dollars. Discounting for inflation, U.S. exports to the LAC countries were stagnant during the 1980s, reflecting the economic stagnation in the countries themselves.

The U.S. interest goes beyond trade as such. The United States is the leading foreign investor in the Western Hemisphere. This is particularly true in Canada and Mexico, but prevails as well in the rest of the hemisphere. Trade has followed investment. Earlier, during the import-substitution period in the hemisphere, U.S. investment in manufacturing was designed largely to serve the protected domestic market in the host country. This was attractive in the countries with the larger economies, such as Canada, Mexico, and Brazil, but less so in the smaller economies.

Today, as trade barriers are coming down, U.S. multinational corporations or MNCs have a substantial interest in coproduction arrangements in the Western Hemisphere. The very basis for the export-processing zones that have proliferated in the LAC countries, especially in Mexico, the Caribbean, and Central America, is to exploit factor advantages – primarily low labor costs for labor-intensive operations – available in these countries. Their proximity minimizes transportation costs. These arrangements involving the shipment of intermediate goods across national boundaries require low trade barriers.

Although the United States thus has a combined trade and production interest in a WHFTA, this cannot be based on giving up markets in other regions because, as table 3-1 shows, U.S. merchandise exports are broadly equally divided among three regions – the Western Hemisphere, Asia and the Pacific, and Western Europe. This division of U.S. exports provides an incentive to keep import barriers against third countries relatively low even if economic integration flourishes in the Americas.

Given that the U.S. interest in free trade in this hemisphere is based on potential long-term dynamic economic benefits, the prospective economic gains for the United States in a WHFTA are not overwhelming. The biggest potential economic gains are in North America, and NAFTA already exists. The only other potentially large, emerging market is Brazil, whose position on acceding to NAFTA or signing a bilateral free trade agreement with the United States is problematic.

Based solely on economics, my view is that the United States can either take or leave the notion of a WHFTA. The impetus for President Bush's proposal came more from political and historical considerations. This is the hemisphere in which the United States is located. This fact stimulated the Alliance for Progress in the 1960s, just as earlier it had Franklin Roosevelt's Good Neighbor Policy. Is this adequate reason for a WHFTA from the U.S. viewpoint? Possibly not, by itself. But this rationale goes with the economic promise and the combination has some force.

The Canadian Interest

The Canadian interest in Western Hemisphere free trade is even less evident than that of the United States. Excluding Mexico, with which Canada already has a free trade agreement, only about 2 percent of Canadian exports go to LAC countries. The Canadian case has been referred to as "reluctant regionalism."[12] Canada joined the NAFTA negotiations to protect its interests in the U.S. market, but did so with considerable misgiving. Canada is being drawn into the broader regional free trade process for much the same reason, to protect its trade position in the United States and its potential interests more broadly in LAC countries, plus the desire to prevent a hub-and-spoke outcome. The phrase hub-and-spoke as it refers to hemispheric free trade originated in Canada and is heard more from Canadian sources – governmental, academic, and business – than from elsewhere in the hemisphere. Indeed, as table 5-1 shows, LAC countries are quite prepared to move ahead on a hub-and-spoke basis when they are the hubs; Mexico is particularly conspicuous in this respect. The Canadian position against a hub-and-spoke outcome in the Western Hemisphere is, in my view, the correct one.

The hub-and-spoke terminology refers to one hub country having separate bilateral free trade agreements with a number of other countries – the spokes – while the latter do not have free trade with each other. The hub country would then be the most attractive for investment and would have preferential treatment in spoke-country markets that the spokes did not enjoy among themselves. The terminology and analysis come from a Canadian economist, Ronald Wonnacott.[13]

However reluctant Canada's regionalism may be, the process, if it prospers, will have repercussions on that country's future trade and investment policy in the hemisphere. Western Europe was not seen as a natural trading area before the establishment of the European Economic Community, but the EU is seen now as being a quite natural trading bloc. This "natural" trading area is growing throughout Europe by grafting additional countries onto the EU. The preferential opportunities that freer trade in the Western Hemisphere can provide should serve as a stimulus to Canadian businesses to invest more in LAC countries and to exploit export opportunities. It would be a mistake to assume that past Canadian lack of interest in most of the LAC region would prevail in the future if circumstances changed. In years past, Canada yearned for what was called the "third option," which was based on expanding exports to Europe and Japan and thereby reducing dependence on the U.S. market.[14] This failed, but Latin America may turn out to be Canada's third option.

The LAC Interest

Defining the LAC interest is more complex than for either Canada or the United States because of the differences among LAC countries. Mexico has a natural market in the United States, one that has been nurtured over the years by U.S. investment and coproduction and regional marketing alliances. This interest is reflected in the creation of NAFTA—but not necessarily in the creation of a WHFTA. The more countries in the hemisphere that have free access to the U.S. market, the more Mexican preferences will be diluted. Yet, for political and cultural reasons, Mexico has muted any misgivings about being joined in free trade by other LAC countries.

The first approach to the LAC interest in a WHFTA is to examine the current destination of exports. How much goes to the United States, and how much to other LAC countries? Such an examination would lead to the conclusion that the countries that should have the greatest interest in free entry into the U.S. market are Mexico, the Caribbean and Central American countries, Venezuela, Colombia, and to some extent Brazil. The Venezuelan case is tenuous, however, because most of its exports to the

United States are petroleum, for which an FTA is not particularly relevant. Less than 20 percent of Colombia's exports to the United States are manufactured goods, and it is for these products that free trade is most important.

Yet Chile was the first country to seek to join NAFTA, despite the fact that the proportion of its exports to the United States is still relatively low—less than 15 percent normally. Argentina has expressed a similar interest, and it, too, does not send a large percentage of its exports to the United States—in its case, the proportion is normally about 10 percent. In other words, the response of LAC countries to free trade with the United States is based on much more than the current destination of their exports. It is based as well on how they would like to see their economies develop in the future.

A second approach is to examine the extent of tariff and nontariff barriers LAC exports face in the U.S. market. Such an examination leads Refik Erzan and Alexander Yeats to conclude that the countries exporting a wide range of manufactures, such as Mexico and Brazil, should have the greatest interest in removing U.S. tariffs; but those countries exporting raw materials, which face relatively few tariff barriers, are likely to have only a modest interest in free trade with the United States.[15] John Whalley also concludes that there are small incentives for most Latin American countries in an expanded NAFTA.[16]

These approaches—that is, looking at current trade patterns or levels of U.S. protection against current imports from LAC countries—although valid, do not tell the full story. The Canada-U.S. FTA would not have been necessary if the purpose were simply to reduce trade barriers because they were already low. These approaches do not explain the interest of countries like Chile and Argentina. It is more germane to look at the desired composition of exports rather than the current situation. The composition of Mexico's exports changed radically from the early 1980s, when petroleum dominated, to the situation today, when manufactures dominate. The change in domestic development policy in Mexico made the past a poor predictor of the future. The Canadian and Mexican initiatives for free trade with the United States were taken to ensure continuity of U.S. policy, to provide a psychological incentive for foreign investment, and to link their production and marketing closely to the United States.

What's in it for the LAC countries to have free trade with the United States – and with their neighbors in their own subregions as well? I would answer the question by approaching the issue from the viewpoint of domestic development strategies. Country after country in the hemisphere has concluded that its development requires substantial structural adjustment. This obviously involves many aspects of macro- and microeconomic policies, which will differ country by country. One aspect of these new development policies is to induce greater competition through more open markets. These new policies are designed to expand exports. And it is this aspiration that is driving the desire for economic integration, including with the United States.

The Central American and Caribbean countries represent a special case because of their dependence on the U.S. market. Most of these countries now enjoy preferential treatment for their exports to the United States under the Caribbean Basin Initiative (CBI). Under NAFTA, these preferences will have to be shared with Mexico, and under a WHFTA with other countries in South America. Many of the manufactured products they now export come from export-processing zones and pay duty only on the in-country value added when imported by the United States. This benefit would be diluted as other countries obtained duty-free entry for their products entering the United States; or, perhaps more significantly, as the United States gradually eliminates textile and clothing quotas for Mexico under NAFTA. The U.S. quota limitations that exist under the multifiber arrangement in the GATT are scheduled to be phased out over 10 years under the Uruguay Round agreement in any event.

Yet I do not believe the trade problems of the CBI countries should be resolved by accession to NAFTA if these countries are not ready to undertake NAFTA's obligations. An alternative solution is to augment the one-way preferences they now receive under the CBI to avoid disadvantaging them with respect to Mexico.

Getting There

Preferential regional arrangements create incentives for outsiders to get inside, as seen already in the Americas. After the Canada-U.S. FTA was in place, Mexico suggested an FTA with the United States. Chile then requested membership, followed by Colombia and others. The current EU, which started as a community of 6, may be a community of 16 by the start of 1995, if approval is given by the electorates in the 4 EFTA applicant countries.

The initiative on how to proceed with NAFTA's future development — both its consolidation and its widening — rests primarily with the United States, but also with its two NAFTA partners. The following are five broad options, listed first and then discussed in turn. Some of them are mutually exclusive, but others are not. (I use the word "broad" because there are clearly permutations of these options. The preferences expressed are mine.)

1. Consolidate NAFTA first. Delay expansion until NAFTA has been deepened much more than is now the case.

2. Be prepared to make an exception to the first option by negotiating the adherence of Chile. A suboption is to decide whether the United States should negotiate for a bilateral agreement with Chile or for Chile's accession to NAFTA itself.

3. Chile aside, negotiate with other subregional groupings as a unit (for example, with MERCOSUR) or with individual countries of these groupings (for example, Argentina). I prefer the former.

4. Consider interim solutions. Accession to NAFTA by other countries in the hemisphere will take time—because of unwillingness or a lack of readiness to negotiate now, or because U.S. politics is not ripe for substantial expansion of NAFTA. Consideration must be given to what is done in the interim with the realization that the provisional can of course become permanent.

5. Permit NAFTA to expand to include nonhemispheric countries, particularly in Asia and the Pacific. My preference is to delay this.

Consolidate NAFTA First

The rationale for this option is that the admission of new countries before NAFTA itself is consolidated in the manner discussed in chapter 4 would change the very nature of the agreement. Chile may be able to meet the obligations set out in the NAFTA agreement, but not many other LAC countries can. Even for Chile, some derogations may be required, such as on investment issues. Both Mexico and Canada have the right to screen takeovers above a certain value, which is not true for the United States, but this asymmetry is modest.

Major departures from the agreement by acceding countries would inevitably lead to a wider preferential area, but a weak form of integration. The resulting weak agreements would in my opinion not endure because of the clamor that would impel others to want to get inside as well. NAFTA would then become just another instrument for rewarding transitory political allies.

The EU experience is instructive in considering the choice between deepening and widening. Deepening in the Western Hemisphere does not have the same content as it did in Europe, a point already discussed in chapters 2 and 4, but the processes in the two regions can be compared.[17] The EU (and its predecessors, the EEC and the EC) insisted that new entrants commit themselves to the obligations that the existing members had undertaken. The negotiation, other than for the financial arrangements, was then mostly about the transition period. The EU deepened, then widened, then deepened and widened again. The most recent manifestation was the deepening that occurred when the Maastricht Treaty of 1992 set out the objective of economic and monetary union (EMU) – a truly deep commitment if fully carried out – and it was after this that four EFTA countries negotiated for accession. These countries – Austria, Finland, Norway, and Sweden – already had free trade with the EU, but they were not on the inside when major decisions on other aspects of the EU were made. Deepening, in other words, may not be a deterrent to accession; it has not been in the EU.

Negotiate with Chile

Chile is on all the lists as the next entrant into NAFTA, although all the hurdles have not been cleared. The substantive rationale is that Chile, because of the economic restructuring already undertaken and the return to democracy after the dictatorship of Augusto Pinochet, is ready to accept the obligations of the agreement.

Nevertheless, the case for the admission of Chile has weaknesses. Chile is not a major trading partner for the United States. U.S. exports to Chile were $2.6 billion in 1993, not a paltry sum, but only large enough for Chile to rank thirty-third among U.S. export destinations. It is far from the United States and this stretches the meaning of "regional" integration. The kinds of issues that arise within North America – customs along a common border, migration, cross-border environmental pollution – do not arise. Coproduction possibilities are not promising both because of distance and Chile's modest industrial structure. Because Chile is not a member of any broader subregional integration arrangement, other than its FTA with Mexico, the United States gains no platform there from which to penetrate other LAC markets.

Chile is first on the list of potential new entrants because of its economic policy and performance – and because two U.S. presidents, George Bush and Bill Clinton, have stated that Chile is next. The case for Chile is that it would serve as a model for subsequent accession negotiations. If the transition period were modest and Chile more or less signed on to NAFTA as written, or as it exists when Chile accedes, similar conditions can be set for others.

But the Chile as surrogate argument cuts both ways. Under the leadership of Congressman Richard Gephardt, the leader of the Democratic Party in the U.S. House of Representatives, a number of Democrats in the House have suggested that the United States negotiate bilaterally with Chile rather than for accession to NAFTA. The reasoning is that the environmental and labor provisions obtained in the body of NAFTA and in the supplemental agreements do not go far enough. They do not contain, for example, obligations on the right to organize unions or bargain collectively. Gephardt and others reason that these obligations can be strengthened in a bilateral agreement and even be included in the text of the FTA agreement itself, not in side agreements.

On the other side of the political aisle, Republican Party supporters of NAFTA have stated that establishing multinational environmental, labor, and other institutions as part of a trade agreement is anathema to them. The Clinton administration is caught in the middle. It is damned if it accepts either position, and, as a consequence, has punted for the time being.

Using the bilateral and not the NAFTA accession route would, I am convinced, be a disaster for U.S. and hemispheric trade policy. If the United States concluded a bilateral agreement with Chile, Canada has said it would do the same to link the two spokes to the U.S. hub. Canada might well go further and sign bilateral agreements more broadly; in other words, there is a danger of competitive bilateralism in the name of economic integration.

Consider the model that a bilateral agreement with

Chile could establish. The United States would maintain NAFTA, but new FTAs would be bilateral. First would come Chile; Canada would then sign its bilateral with Chile to avoid prejudice to its economic interests. Mexico already has a bilateral FTA with Chile. Then, using the Chile agreement as a model, the United States might sign another bilateral agreement with, say, Argentina. To protect their positions, Canada, perhaps Mexico, and possibly Chile would sign their own bilaterals to protect their own interests. Then would come Colombia and so on and on. Each agreement could have its own technical conditions, not only on labor and the environment but on rules of origin, and they may not coincide with each other. The only saving grace to such a scenario is that U.S. traders and investors would eventually rebel against the complexity, and chaos could then give way to sanity. But is it necessary to court chaos?

There is some history to support this scenario. The United States from the time of its creation as a country until 1923 practiced the policy of conditional most-favored-nation (MFN) – that is, it discriminated against countries unless they gave trade concessions in separate bilateral agreements. Each bilateral had its own provisions on tariff and other arrangements. The main reason for the shift from this conditional MFN to the current policy of unconditional MFN was that as the United States became a major trading nation, the discrimination inherent in this policy generated substantial political conflict. Viner noted that the conditional application of the MFN clause

> has probably been the cause in the last century of more diplomatic controversy, more variations in construction, more international ill-feeling, more conflict between international obligations and municipal law and between judicial interpretation and executive practice, more confusion and uncertainty of operation, than have developed under all the unconditional most-favored-nations pledges of all other countries combined.[18]

A bilateral approach to discrimination in the name of Western Hemisphere economic integration has the same underlying rationale as the old conditional MFN – to distinguish among countries, to deal with Mexico and Canada in one fashion and other countries in the Americas in another. What is needed, instead, is a sorting out of the current mishmash of trading arrangements – including Mexico's own bilateral agreements – in the interest of simplifying economic interaction.

Negotiate by Country or Subregion

There is no clear policy, either in the United States or the LAC countries, as to whether accession to NAFTA should be country-by-country or subregion-to-subregion. The impression left by both sides is allow this issue to play itself out over time – to make policy by facts as they emerge rather than by design. The evidence for this conclusion is the action being taken by the United States to reach partial agreements, such as tax treaties on a country basis, plus the statement in an internal memorandum from the office of the U.S. Trade Representative that this issue should be dealt with by "continuous progressive expansion."[19] On the LAC side, the defections from subregional groupings either to sign free trade agreements with countries outside the subregions or to suggest joining NAFTA indicates that it is each country for itself. Entry into NAFTA by Chile would not resolve this issue because, other than ALADI, Chile is not a member of any subregional grouping.

My preference would be to approach wider hemispheric integration by subregions and not by countries. Just as it weakens NAFTA for the member countries to defect and reach their own bilateral free trade agreements with outside countries, so too does defection weaken the other subregional integration agreements. Competitive bilateralism is no more attractive in Latin America than it is in North America.

Yet it is necessary to understand the reasoning for actual or potential defections from subregional partners. Colombia and Venezuela, to move faster on their integration than is possible within the framework of the five-country Andean pact, created their own bilateral integration arrangement within the larger one. This is understandable, even though the trade engendered by this bilateral is not overwhelming. These two countries then opened negotiations with Mexico for a G-3 free trade area. This is less understandable in terms of subregional integration. Colombia later indicated its desire to accede to NAFTA; this has all the earmarks of abandonment of the Andean group.

Argentina has stated that it may request entry into NAFTA. This action, if taken, could spell the end of MERCOSUR as now envisaged.[20] There is some indication, however, that Argentina's flirtation with NAFTA is a way to prod Brazil to alter economic policy to make MERCOSUR more effective. The president of Uruguay, Luis Alberto Lacalle, is on record against individual defections from MERCOSUR. As he told the *Financial Times*, "The integration movement in Latin America must be modular and step by step. When you think of MERCOSUR, it is made real by geography."[21]

Each subregion must decide its priorities: whether subregional integration should come first, or whether accession to NAFTA is more important. I believe subregional integration will be more important in the long term. The subregional groupings of LAC countries may wish to pursue their own versions of deepening. Much of this would be lost if entry into NAFTA took place country by country. Beyond that, if the NAFTA countries showed little interest in widening their preferential area – something that is clearly possible – subregional integration would have its own rewards.

There is another option to a single WHFTA that could lead to hemispheric free trade without compromising the potential for deepening within subregions where geography and physical infrastructure make a difference. This would be a series of free trade agreements between NAFTA and other subregional groupings when they are ready for this. Under this choice, two subregional groupings – NAFTA, for example, with other LAC subregional groupings – with different obligations among their member countries would seek to reach free trade. This would not obligate either grouping to accept the other's internal arrangements other than those related to border barriers and obligations stemming from this. It is, in rough form, the model that was followed in Europe between the EC and EFTA. The groupings could eventually come together if developments led in that direction, but this would not be necessary.

The disadvantage of this approach is that it would create a new labyrinth of FTAs, but the structure would be much more straightforward than what now exists. After all, the EC and EFTA had separate provisions, but free trade between them; now EFTA is disappearing as its members seek entry into a deepened EU.

These two ways of approaching hemispheric free trade would almost certainly lead to different outcomes. The first approach of looking toward a single WHFTA would subordinate other subregional arrangements in the sense that they would have to abide by NAFTA provisions. Under this scenario, they would become redundant and probably would wither away.

The second approach would allow each subregion to develop according to its own idiosyncrasies, but could still lead to free trade between it and NAFTA, and between it and other subregions. Other subregional agreements – that is, other than NAFTA – also have the potential to deepen well beyond trade matters – into other economic areas, transportation, and policy consultation. Effective subregionalism does not preclude preferential trade with the countries of North America. If anything, deeper subregional integration will enhance the bargaining power of the subregions.

A series of FTAs among regional groupings would simplify the maze of integration arrangements that now exist if it were made clear that individual countries could join only one subregional arrangement. If individual countries continue to have multiple subregional memberships, this can only complicate the current complexity of trade relationships.

The suggestion that NAFTA not accept individual country applications for accession if this threatens the existence of other subregional groupings may be like trying to hold back the whirlwind. But it may happen by default if NAFTA entry is long delayed because of political considerations both in the United States and elsewhere in the hemisphere. In that case, strengthening the promising subregional arrangements would be the most promising of available options.

Consider Interim Solutions

Perhaps the most urgent issue that needs resolution is not the procedure for the accession to NAFTA, but rather what should or can be done between now and the time that happens – if it does occur. The United States is not ready for wholesale accession to NAFTA. Mexico seems intent on widening its preferential trade, not on diluting its preferential treatment in the U.S. market. Canada is unsure what it should do to reduce its trade reliance on the United States. And, perhaps most crucial, few Latin American and Caribbean countries are ready to join NAFTA, and many are not sure they will ever wish to do so.

Yet, just about all LAC countries want a close trade relationship with the United States, as was evident from the reception to President Bush's EAI. The issue is to square this circle – if not NAFTA accession, or at least not yet, then what?

A procedure similar to that adopted by the EC might be followed. The EC offered trade benefits to countries that relied heavily on its market but were unable to undertake the deep commitments demanded of member countries. The extent of these benefits and the form they took varied case by case. They included free trade with EFTA countries, free trade with Israel, better trade access by the Maghreb countries in North Africa, discussions of a similar nature with countries in Eastern Europe, and one-way trade preferences to African-Caribbean-Pacific (ACP) countries under the various Lomé agreements.

The obligations undertaken were greatest at the center, among member countries of the EC, and weaker for countries furthest from the center – that is, weaker for the ACP countries than for the EFTA countries. Similarly, the potential benefits were greatest for countries at the center. This has been referred to as the concentric-circle approach.[22] Another analyst has made roughly the same suggestion to define classes of membership in NAFTA – full or associate membership – depending on the degree of commitment and, consequently, of benefits.[23]

What might these different arrangements be in NAFTA? Some are already in place, at least in part. The United States provides special trade benefits to CBI and Andean countries; Canada does the same for some Caribbean countries. The United States could go further and offer parity of treatment with Mexico for CBI countries in products crucial to that region's economy, such as textile products. The understandings can be in specific functional areas, such as tax treaties to avoid double taxation and technical assistance. The arrangements might contain provisions to facilitate dispute-settlements. The suggestion for FTAs between NAFTA and other subregional integration arrangements is a form of associate membership.

Such agreements can be reciprocal, as long as they do not violate the GATT. Thus, preferential sectoral agreements should be taboo. In return for better access to NAFTA markets, however, countries might be asked to make commitments on an MFN basis freeing trade in services, liberalizing investment restrictions, and providing more protection for intellectual property.

I believe such an approach is possible. This would be a way to minimize harm to nonmembers of NAFTA from trade and investment diversion without compromising the deepening of integration in North America.

Expand to Nonhemispheric Countries

NAFTA's accession provision, article 2204, has no geographic limitation. There is much support in the United States for expanding NAFTA, or possibly to use bilateral U.S. FTAs, with Asian countries because of the high growth rates and promising markets that exist there.

In my view, nonregional countries should not be excluded in principle, but the decision should be deferred until the process in the hemisphere has progressed much further than it has to date. Expansion of free trade to Asian countries raises both economic and political problems. The trade and investment policies of many East Asian countries are not now compatible with the NAFTA structure. Beyond that, seeking preferential trade in the region dominated by Japan would be akin to a declaration of economic war. I recommend that the United States confine its NAFTA-widening efforts to this hemisphere for now. It is still possible to further penetrate Asian markets by traditional, nonpreferential methods.

Institutional Arrangements

One rule of institution building should be kept in mind: Do not create institutions in the hope that a new body will lead to creative thinking. It is better when uncertain to think first, then act. There is no shortage of hemispheric and regional institutions that can be used in the interim, such as the Inter-American Development Bank (IDB), the Economic Commission for Latin America and the Caribbean (ECLAC), the Organization of American States (OAS) , the Latin American Economic System (SELA), which excludes the United States, and the various secretariats of the sub-regional integration groupings.

If the architecture chosen for hemispheric free trade is to seek a single WHFTA by building on the core of NAFTA, this path would require one type of institutional structure. If, instead, the choice is to reach free trade by a series of FTAs, then quite different kinds of institutions would be needed. In the first case, the organization needed would be similar to those of other large integration arrangements. It would require, at a minimum: a secretariat for monitoring the daily operations of WHFTA, carrying out studies, making proposals, and preparing positions for negotiations within WHFTA and with other countries and groupings; a policy- and rule-making body for making decisions; and many panels or a single body for dispute resolution.

If the emphasis is to strengthen subregional groupings in the hemisphere, which may some day coalesce, a large, unified secretariat would not be called for, certainly not for now. Instead, each subregional grouping would function with its own secretariat, but with coordinating functions among the various groupings for cross consistency of the FTAs. Existing institutions like the OAS, the IDB, and ECLAC could be drawn on for more comprehensive studies, if so desired. There are many variations between these two structures, just as there are substantive variations on the nature of integration in the hemisphere.

Conclusion

What is noteworthy is that this chapter was even necessary. A discussion about widening the integration effort in the Americas, one that would include North America as well as the rest of the hemisphere, would have been superfluous five years ago.

It is not inevitable that hemispheric free trade will occur. The successful conclusion of the Uruguay Round gave much stimulus to multilateral trade opening, and the GATT route can be pursued in future rounds of trade negotiations without a simultaneous drive toward hemispheric free trade. The subregional groupings in the LAC region are stronger than ever, particularly the most important of them, MERCOSUR. These groupings can strengthen further without ever coming together. The Brazilians have proposed the formation of a South American free trade region. This offers less in trade potential than hemispheric free trade, but it is an option. Finally, the unilateral opening of markets that has been typical of the LAC region during the last decade has not reached its limit. Countries can continue this process further, although this would not necessarily lead to the reciprocal further opening of the U.S. and Canada markets.

Each of these options, however, offers less than hemispheric free trade. Worldwide market opening through future GATT negotiations, although desirable, will surely be slower and less comprehensive in terms of hemispheric economic commitments. Subregional markets within the LAC region are promising, but relatively limited. And unilateral market opening does not cover both sides of the trade picture as fully as mutual openings.

Why is hemispheric free trade now an option? The answer is in the nature of the development philosophy that has emerged in the LAC region. Countries are opening their markets and seeking to promote exports, with or without free trade. The process of achieving free trade requires that the countries of the hemisphere make value judgments of what they would like to reject or include in the final arrangements that emerge. I offer my judgments on these matters with the hope that they assist governments in developing their own positions.

6

Conclusion

Profound change has occurred in the international economy during the past several decades to which the United States and other countries of this hemisphere must adapt. Change crept onto the scene almost unnoticed. Capital movements across borders, which have long exceeded the movement of goods, have now exploded. The gap between the international movement of goods and of capital continues to widen, with no end in sight. The United States cannot isolate itself from the computer and split-second global communication that make possible the transfer of trillions of dollars of capital around the globe.

Trade in goods has not stood still; indeed, it has grown by much more than production – another manifestation of the hopelessness of economic isolation. The trade that is growing most rapidly is between firms in the same industry (intraindustry trade) and within the same firm (intrafirm trade). The United States exports computers and parts as well as importing them. There are more U.S. exports of automotive products to Mexico and Canada than of goods in any other sector, and these same products are the most important U.S. imports from these countries. The global division of production under which parts of final goods are made in various countries facilitates the exploitation of those features that abound in different locations. These might be, among other factors, cheap labor, the availability of skilled technicians, or convenience of transportation. Specialization permits building economies of scale into the production process.

The biggest increases of merchandise trade in recent years have been in intermediate goods, the inputs that go into final products. Where is an automobile made? All over, really. Is Toyota a Japanese product? Yes. Is it a U.S. product? The answer is again yes.[1] The same situation exists for U.S. automotive production, as well as for the manufacture of computers, pharmaceuticals, machinery, chemicals, textiles, and other goods. To bring all this intermediate production home to the United States risks starting a trade war that would reduce both world and U.S. welfare. The United States cannot export either finished or intermediate products to the extent it does without importing these same kinds of products from others. There is no costless way to get off the world. It is this recognition that led to the change in economic policy of other countries in this hemisphere; and it is this reality that stimulates talk of hemispheric economic integration.

The change in trading relationships goes well beyond the growth in intraindustry and intrafirm transactions between the United States and its traditional trading partners. There are new actors on the world scene, and they will not go away. They will only multiply, and the United States is powerless to stop this evolution. The Asian tigers, those that exist already and others that are emerging, are catching up. Mexico is catching up, as is Brazil.

The famous remark of Satchel Paige is relevant: "Don't look back. Something may be gaining on you." The United States can withdraw from the race, or try to stay ahead. It can stay ahead only by higher productivity, more innovation, improved technology, and by developing an increasingly educated and skilled population. Protectionism is withdrawal. It can conserve jobs in those activities that others can do better, but at the expense of advances in fields in which we can excel.

The foregoing discussion is phrased in terms of the production of goods, which is a declining proportion of total output. Services now provide nearly 80 percent of non-farm U.S. jobs. One recent study concluded that in 1992 the average weekly wage for full-time service workers was only 3.9 percent below the average goods-producing wage.[2] In 1993, U.S. service exports were equal to 36 percent of U.S. merchandise exports. Unlike its trade in goods, the United States has a surplus in its services trade with the rest of the world. The elementary fact that trade no longer deals only with the movement of goods across borders, but also of services, also makes evident how difficult it would be to practice protectionism. If the United States tries to keep out the goods of other countries, so too can they keep out U.S. competitive service exports.

World trade, in both goods and services, is growing more rapidly within major world regions than between them. For the United States, this reality emerges most clearly in trade with its two land neighbors, Canada and Mexico. The United States, therefore, has a major stake in the economic health of its neighbors; and not just Canada and Mexico, but also the rest of the Western Hemisphere, where the United States is the leading supplier of the region's imports, as it is not for the other major regions, either Asia or Europe. NAFTA is a way to put stress on neighborhood, as is the proposal for wider free trade in the Americas.

Finally, one other manifestation of the economic changes that are taking place and that must be factored into U.S. policy is what can be labeled as a paradigm shift in the LAC region. Until the decade of the 1980s, the so-called tragic decade in which LAC economies plummeted, the LAC countries looked inward. They protected their internal markets and downgraded the economic growth that could be generated from exports. The phrase used to describe the latter was "export pessimism"; the argument was that if the region's exports did grow, the producers in the importing countries, the industrialized nations, would find ways to restrict this growth.

LAC now looks outward. National markets are now

protected by only modest border barriers. FDI, once eschewed, is now actively sought. The MNCs are no longer seen as the enemy, but as potential allies who can bring capital, technology, production skills, and marketing talents. In many respects, the LAC countries have become more convinced of the virtue of open markets than the United States. It is they who have unilaterally reduced their import restrictions to augment export competitiveness. The United States, by contrast, is locked into a philosophy of reciprocity; it does others a favor by giving them access to the U.S. market, and this requires some favor in return. The pupils have overtaken the master professor.

The very fact that this book could be written and taken seriously is itself remarkable. Who could have contemplated a generation ago that the LAC region would shed its protectionism, reduce the extent of government involvement in production, discard its export pessimism, and even consider entering into FTAs with the United States? It may not be possible to achieve a WHFTA in the foreseeable future, but the fact that this objective is even on the hemisphere's agenda is astounding.

Hope and Pessimism

To contemplate the future of hemispheric relations evokes a mixture of hope and pessimism. The reasons for hope are manifold. The countries of the Americas are responding to the changed world scene. All of them – including the United States – are fundamentally restructuring their economies to adapt to current world production realities. They are not trying to stifle capital flows, as the LAC countries did for FDI until the 1980s, but are actively seeking them. Closed markets have opened, and the drive is to open them more. Destructive forms of nationalism, those which stressed xenophobia, are being discarded. The United States had been vilified as predatory, as an economic imperialist, for most of the period after World War

II. It is now sought as a free trade partner. Subregional integration that earlier had taken the form of widening the area for protectionism has given way to open regionalism.

With NAFTA in place, the debate now focuses on what comes next. This is a sea change in U.S. interaction with its neighbors, as it is for the two neighbors in their relations with the United States.

But there are grounds for pessimism. The Americas have come this far, but now hesitate—especially the United States. Fears of lost sovereignty have been most strident here, not in weaker countries where one would expect this concern to be greatest. The Clinton administration is caught between those who would expand economic relations with the hemisphere by reverting to a form of bilateralism that for good reason was jettisoned more than 60 years ago, and others who have drawn a line in the sand that integration refers only to trade and such related issues as investment, but nothing more—not environmental protection, not working conditions in countries with which the United States trades. The political scene in the United States is tailor-made for stalemate.

Other countries in the hemisphere are having second thoughts. The adjustment to the new world situation has not created a bed of roses, certainly not yet. It is not clear that the economic lot of the majority of the people in the LAC countries has worsened since the change in the economic development model, but signs of improvement are still modest on a hemispheric basis. The depression in most countries of the hemisphere during the 1980s was the last hurrah of the old, inward-looking, state-led model, but cause and effect get twisted when changes do not lead to immediate satisfaction. There are thus signs of restructuring fatigue in countries such as Venezuela and Costa Rica. Brazil, the most important country in South America, is unsure of what it wishes its future policy to be.

The remaining countries of the hemisphere are looking to the United States for leadership. They desire a set of principles that can foster deeper economic cooperation in the Americas. They do not know how to articulate the principles, but hope the United States can provide the guidance. The hemisphere is now almost completely democratic. And although many of the democracies are frail, this is indeed a unique moment.

The problem is that the United States is most unsure of where it wants to lead, or even that it wishes to do so. Does it wish to intrude or to cooperate? Is it prepared to foster economic integration, or does it intend to slow down the process?

The current situation of general concord in economic and political philosophy is without precedent in relations between the United States and the rest of the hemisphere. It would be an error of monumental proportions to let the opportunity fizzle out in disappointment – an error that need not happen.

Notes

Chapter 1

1. The themes listed in the text are called for in the text of NAFTA. Other necessary micro decisions will grow out of the operations of the free-trade area.

2. Robert Kasten, "Regulatory Tide high and rising," *Washington Times*, January 11, 1994, p. A15.

3. This very issue came to the surface on New Year's Day 1994, when the self-styled Zapatista National Liberation Army rose up violently in the state of Chiapas in Mexico. One of the questions raised in the United States was whether the first reaction of the federal government in Mexico in its forceful suppression of the rebel movement violated the human rights of the mostly indigenous insurgents. Congressional hearings were held on whether Mexico was suitably democratic for the free-trade agreement that came into effect on the day of the uprising. My view is that the federal government changed its policy from suppressing the rebels to negotiating with them largely because of the scrutiny of Mexico brought on by NAFTA (a theme developed later in the text).

4. CUFTA went into effect on January 1, 1989, and the Canadian dollar shortly thereafter soared to near parity with the U.S. dollar — a consequence of domestic macroeconomic policy in Canada. By the end of 1993, the Canadian dollar had fallen to less than 75 cents in relation to the U.S. dollar. The value of the

Mexican peso appreciated gradually after 1987, and what a few years ago was undervaluation in relation to the U.S. dollar shifted to substantial overvaluation by early 1994. Following the assassination of Luis Donaldo Colosio, the PRI candidate for president, the peso depreciated again. The simple point is that exchange-rate relationships among the North American currencies have shown much variability during the last five years.

Chapter 2

1. Jagdish Bhagwati, *The World Trading System at Risk* (Princeton, N.J.: Princeton University Press, 1991). A variant of the term "aggressive unilateralism" is "aggressive reciprocity," used by William Cline in "'Reciprocity': A New Approach to Trade Policy?" in Cline, ed., *Trade Policy in the 1980s* (Washington, D.C.: Institute for International Economics, 1983), 121–158.

2. Dumping technically refers to selling products at less than fair value. In practice, it is used against foreign companies when they exercise price discrimination by selling products for less in the U.S. market than in their home or third-country markets. The GATT trade policy review of the United States (C/RM/S/45 of 19 January 1994, p. 51) shows that the number of antidumping investigations initiated by the United States increased from 24 between July 1989 and June 1990 to 74 between July 1992 and June 1993.

3. *Economic Report of the President* (Washington, D.C.: U.S. Government Printing Office, 1994), 206; and export data for 1993 from the U.S. Department of Commerce.

4. Russell B. Scholl, Jeffrey H. Lowe, and Sylvia Bargas, "The International Investment Position of the United States in 1992," *Survey of Current Business* 73, no. 6 (June 1993): 49.

5. "U.S. Direct Investment Abroad: Detail for Historical-Cost Position and Balance of Payments Flows, 1992," *Survey of Current Business* 73, no. 7 (July 1993): 91.

6. For example, see Adolfo Aguilar Zinser, "Challenges to NAFTA from a Mexican Perspective," *Looking Ahead* (quarterly opinion publication of the National Planning Association) 15, no. 2 (July 1993): 23–26.

7. Raymond J. Mataloni, Jr., "U.S. Multinational Companies: Operations in 1991," *Survey of Current Business* 73, no. 7 (July 1993): 45–47.

8. William J. Zeile, "Merchandise Trade of U.S. Affiliates of Foreign Companies," *Survey of Current Business* 73, no. 10 (October 1993): 52.

9. Ralph Nader, "Introduction: Free Trade and the Decline of Democracy," in Nader et al., *The Case against Free Trade: GATT, NAFTA, and the Globalization of Corporate Power* (San Francisco: Earth Island Press, and Berkeley: North Atlantic Books, 1993), 8.

10. Mataloni, "U.S. Multinational Corporations," 49.

11. Scholl, Lowe, and Bargas, "The International Investment Position of the United States in 1992," 51.

12. World Bank, *World Development Report 1993* (New York: Oxford University Press, 1993), 238–239.

13. Robert Summers and Alan Heston, "The Penn World Table (Mark 5): An Expanded Set of International Comparisons, 1950–1988," *Quarterly Journal of Economics* 106, no. 2 (May 1991): 353. There are many ways to make purchasing-power-parity comparisons (PPP), which seek to determine what income is required to purchase an identical basket of goods and services as if there were a common currency.

14. Chapter 16 of NAFTA provides for the temporary movement of businesspersons into other member countries, but this is quite different and much more limited than a right of movement of all nationals of member countries.

15. The responsibilities of the Free Trade Commission are set forth in chapter 20. It states that the commission *shall* supervise implementation of the agreement, oversee its elaboration, resolve disputes, supervise the work of committees established in an annex to chapter 20, and consider any other matter that may affect the operation of the agreement. The commission *may* delegate, set up other working groups, seek outside advice, and take other actions as the parties agree. It must meet at least once a year and take decisions by consensus unless the parties otherwise agree.

16. Gert Rosenthal, executive secretary of the Economic Commission for Latin America and the Caribbean, statement on the occasion of the presidential summit of the Rio group, Santiago, Chile, October 16, 1993.

17. This phrase, "open regionalism," means low barriers against outsiders when used in the Americas, but it means no border preferences when used by Japan in reference to its eco-

nomic relations with other countries in East Asia. The usage reflects the pattern on the ground.

Chapter 3

1. Leigh B. Boske, Robert Harrison, Chandler Stolp, and Sidney Weintraub, directors, *Texas-Mexico Multimodal Transportation*, policy research project report no. 104 (Austin: Lyndon B. Johnson School of Public Affairs, University of Texas: 1993), 8.

2. As noted in chapter 2, although Mexico's per capita GDP was then about $3,000 a year measured in the conventional manner of using official exchange-rate relationships, the figure was more than $5,000 on a PPP basis in 1988. The *Economist* estimates Mexican GDP per head in 1991 at $7,170 on a PPP basis (December 25, 1993, p. 39). Timothy J. Kehoe, "Assessing the Economic Impact of North American Free Trade," discussion paper no. 265, Center for Economic Research, University of Minnesota, October 1992, points out that when measured on a PPP, not the conventional, basis, income per capita in the United States is only four times greater than that in Mexico, rather than nine times greater.

3. Calculations are based on trade data from the U.S. Department of Commerce. The trade data are in current dollars.

4. U.S. Embassy, Mexico City, "Mexico: Economic and Financial Report, Winter 1994."

5. Sidney Weintraub, *A Marriage of Convenience: Relations between Mexico and the United States* (New York: Oxford University Press for the Twentieth Century Fund, 1990), 102.

6. U.S. Embassy, Mexico City, "Mexico: Foreign Investment Supplement, January 1994."

7. Michael Hart, *Trade: Why Bother?* (Ottawa: Centre for Trade Policy and Law, 1992), 14.

8. U.S. International Trade Commission, *Potential Impact on the U.S. Economy and Selected Industries of the North American Free-Trade Agreement*, USITC publication 2596 (Washington, D.C.: USITC, January 1993), x.

9. U.S. Department of Commerce, Bureau of Economic Analysis, *U.S. Direct Investment Abroad: Operations of U.S. Parent Companies and Their Foreign Affiliates* (Washington, D.C.: U.S. Government Printing Office, July 1993), tables II.H.5 and II.H.22; and U.S. Department of Commerce, International

Trade Administration, *U.S. Foreign Trade Highlights 1992* (U.S. Government Printing Office, 1993), 28.

10. Figures are from the Banco de México, *Indicadores Económicos*. This is a running compilation of data from the Bank of Mexico, which provides new information monthly.

11. Sidney Weintraub, *The Maquiladora Industry in Mexico: Its Transitional Role*, Commission for the Study of International Migration and Cooperative Economic Development, working paper no. 39, June 1990.

12. The role of the maquiladora system under NAFTA is discussed in U.S. International Trade Commission, *Production Sharing: U.S. Imports under Harmonized Tariff Schedule Provisions 9802.00.60 and 9802.00.80, 1989–1992*, USITC publication 2729 (Washington, D.C.: USITC, February 1994), 3–1 through 4–6.

13. U.S. Department of Labor, Bureau of Labor Statistics, "International Comparisons of Hourly Compensation Costs for Production Workers in Manufacturing, 1992," report 844, April 1993, p. 5.

14. This was the main theme of the Report of the Commission for the Study of International Migration and Cooperative Economic Development, *Unauthorized Migration: An Economic Development Response* (Washington, D.C.: U.S. Government Printing Office, July 1990). The commission was mandated in the Immigration Reform and Control Act of 1986 to address the economic "push" factors that stimulate emigration from Mexico.

15. The vote count can be found in the *Wall Street Journal* of November 18, 1993, for the House of Representatives and in the *Washington Post* of November 21, 1993, for the Senate.

16. Philip L. Martin, *Trade and Migration: NAFTA and Agriculture* (Washington, D.C.: Institute for International Economics, 1993), 3 and 7.

17. Lawrence Katz, statement on "Immigration Issues and the North American Free Trade Agreement," before the subcommittee on International Law, Immigration, and Refugees of the House Judiciary Committee, November 3, 1993.

18. Sherman Robinson, Mary Burfisher, Raul Hinojosa-Ojeda, and Karen Thierfelder, "Agricultural Policies and Migration in a U.S.-Mexico Free Trade Area: A Computable General Equilibrium Analysis," working paper no. 617, Department of Agricultural and Resource Economics, University of California at Berkeley, December 1991.

19. Article by Roberto Suro, "U.S., Mexico Taking Cautious Steps to Address Immigration Issues" *Washington Post*, May 8, 1994, p. A6.

Chapter 4

1. This is the main conclusion of the analysis in Gary Clyde Hufbauer and Jeffrey J. Schott, *NAFTA: An Assessment*, rev. ed. (Washington, D.C.: Institute for International Economics, 1993).

2. Paolo Cecchini, *The European Challenge 1992: The Benefits of a Single Market* (Hants, England: Wildwood House, 1988).

3. See George Kopits, *Tax Harmonization in the European Community*, occasional paper 94 (Washington, D.C.: International Monetary Fund, 1992), 1–21.

4. R.H. Coase, "The Institutional Structure of Production," *American Economic Review* 82, no. 4 (September 1992): 713–719.

5. Ewell E. Murphy, "Opportunities for U.S. Business in Mexico," *Mexico Trade and Law Reporter* 3, no. 12 (December 1993): 12.

6. Boris Kozolchyk, ed., *Toward Seamless Borders: Making Free Trade Work in the Americas* (Tucson: National Law Center for Inter-American Free Trade, 1993).

7. A brief description of this case can be found in C. Ford Runge, *Freer Trade, Protected Environment: Balancing Trade Liberalization and Environmental Interests* (New York: Council on Foreign Relations Press, 1994), 36–37.

8. Another effort to restrict tomato and other fresh fruit and vegetable imports from Mexico was the antidumping case brought by Florida producers in 1978. The final decision favored Mexico. This case is described briefly in Sidney Weintraub, *A Marriage of Convenience*, 83.

9. I have drawn from a paper by Joseph A. Greenwald of November 1993, prepared for the use of the U.S. Council of the Mexico-U.S. Business Committee on the "Opportunities for Business Input in NAFTA Procedures and Groups" for these illustrations of NAFTA provisions.

10. An example of the depth of feeling on this subject can be found in a speech to the Association of American Chambers of Commerce in Latin America on May 5, 1994, in Washington, D.C., by Congressman Jim Kolbe (R-Ariz.). The fourth of his

five principles on establishing a Western Hemisphere Free Trade Area (WHFTA) is that no new hemispheric institutions should be created. Congressman Kolbe is an ardent supporter of NAFTA, as he is of a WHFTA.

11. Richard G. Lipsey, "Getting There: The Path to a Western Hemisphere Free Trade Area and Its Structure," in Sylvia Saborio, ed., *The Premise and the Promise: Free Trade in the Americas* (New Brunswick, N.J.: Transaction Publishers for the Overseas Development Council, 1992), 107.

12. The quotations are from Lloyd Bentsen, U.S. Secretary of the Treasury. The swap line was opened in the wake of the assassination of presidential candidate Luis Donaldo Colosio on March 23, 1994, then made permanent a short time later.

13. A position in favor of monetary union was taken by Richard G. Harris, "Trade, Money and Wealth in the Canadian Economy," C.D. Howe Institute, Benefactors Lecture, September 14, 1993.

14. There are many analyses of U.S. AD and CVD practices. These include Thomas M. Boddez and Michael J. Trebilcock, *Unfinished Business: Reforming Trade Remedy Laws in North America* (Toronto: C.D. Howe, 1993); Pietro S. Nivola, *Regulating Unfair Trade* (Washington, D.C.: Brookings Institution, 1993); and Richard Boltuck and Robert E. Litan, eds., *Down in the Dumps: Administration of the Unfair Trade Laws* (Washington, D.C.: Brookings Institution, 1991).

15. The first description on the unfairness of the unfair trade laws is from the *New York Times*, July 20, 1993, p. C1, in an article by Peter Passel; and the "wacko" assessment is from the *Globe and Mail* of Toronto, June 22, 1993, in an editorial column on steel AD cases.

16. Cathryn L. Thorup, "Redefining Governance in North America: The Impact of Cross-Border Networks and Coalitions on Mexican Immigration into the United States," RAND, DRU-219-FF, March 1993; and Thorup, "Redefining Governance in North America: Citizen Diplomacy and Cross-Border Coalitions," *Enfoque*, Center for U.S.-Mexican Studies, University of California, San Diego, Spring 1993.

17. Sidney Weintraub, "The Rise of North Americanos: A U.S.-Mexico Union," *The Responsive Community* 1, no. 3 (Summer 1991): 64–74.

18. Lucía Luna, "Un Equilibrio Pragmático," *Este País*, no. 27 (June 1993): 2–13.

19. September 22, 1993, p. A25.

20. *Washington Times*, op-ed column, September 22, 1993.

21. Jerry Taylor, "NAFTA's Green Accords: Sound and Fury Signifying Little," Cato Institute policy analysis paper no. 198, November 17, 1993.

22. Letter from Michael Kantor to Representative Bill Archer, ranking Republican member of the Ways and Means Committee of the House of Representatives, as reprinted in *Inside U.S. Trade*, October 22, 1993, p. 16.

23. Luis Rubio and Alain de Remes, *¿Como va a afectar a México el tratado de libre comercio?* (México, D.F.: Fondo de Cultura Económica, 1992), 95 and 284.

Chapter 5

1. Peter Hakim, "President Bush's Southern Strategy: The Enterprise for the Americas Initiative," *Washington Quarterly* 15, no. 2 (Spring 1992): 93, notes that Enrique Iglesias, president of the Inter-American Development Bank, referred to the EAI as perhaps the most ambitious proposal in the LAC region's relations with the United States.

2. This point is made in one form or another by several scholars from the LAC region. See Moisés Naim, a Venezuelan, "Towards Free Trade in the Americas: Building Blocks, Stumbling Blocks and Entry Fees," paper prepared for a conference on the Future of Western Hemisphere Economic Integration sponsored by the Center for Strategic and International Studies, Inter-American Dialogue, and North-South Center of Miami, Washington, D.C., March 2–4, 1994; Patricio Meller, a Chilean, "A Latin American Perspective of NAFTA," Corporación de Investigaciones Económicas para Latinoamerica (CIEPLAN), Santiago, Chile, October 1992; and R. DeLisle Worrell, a Barbadian, "Economic Integration with Unequal Partners: The Caribbean and North America," Woodrow Wilson Center for Scholars, working paper 205, 1994.

3. The summit was proposed initially in a speech by Vice President Al Gore entitled "Toward a Western Hemisphere Community of Democracies," given in Mexico City to the Mexican, American, and Latin American Chambers of Commerce, on December 1, 1993. The December date and Miami location were announced in a White House press release of March 11, 1994.

4. Richard G. Lipsey, "Getting There: The Path to a Western

Hemisphere Free Trade Area and Its Structure," in Sylvia Saborio, ed., *The Premise and the Promise*, makes this same point. "The basic principle for a WHFTA is that there should be *one* free trade agreement" (107, emphasis in original).

5. This point has been endorsed by the U.S. government. See speech by Alexander F. Watson, "Toward a Mature Partnership: U.S.-Latin American relations in the 1990s," speech by Alexander F. Watson, assistant secretary of state for Inter-American Affairs, before the Institute of the Americas, La Jolla, Calif., March 2, 1994.

6. Sidney Weintraub, "Regionalism and the GATT: The North American Initiative," *SAIS Review* 11, no. 1 (Winter–Spring 1991): 46.

7. U.S. Secretary of State James G. Blaine proposed the formation of a hemispheric free-trade area at the Washington Conference of American States in 1889–1890. The suggestion was peremptorily dismissed by the Latin American representatives.

8. Isaac Cohen, "A New Latin American and Caribbean Nationalism," *ANNALS* of the American Academy of Political and Social Sciences (issue on "Free Trade in the Western Hemisphere") 526 (March 1993): 36–46.

9. Figures from Naim, "Towards Free Trade in the Americas."

10. Economic Commission for Latin America and the Caribbean (ECLAC), *Open Regionalism in Latin America and the Caribbean* (Santiago, Chile: United Nations ECLAC, document LC/G.1801 (SES.25/4), 1994), 51.

11. U.S. Department of Commerce, *U.S. Foreign Trade Highlights 1992* (Washington, D.C.: International Trade Administration, 1993), 11.

12. Al Berry, Leonard Waverman, and Ann Weston, "Canada and the Enterprise for the Americas Initiative: A Case of Reluctant Regionalism," *Business Economics* 27, no. 2 (April 1992): 31–38.

13. Ronald J. Wonnacott, *The Economics of Overlapping Free Trade Areas and the Mexican Challenge* (Toronto: C.D. Howe Institute; Washington, D.C.: National Planning Association, 1991).

14. The expression "third option" came from a policy paper in the 1970s, which listed options for Canada's future trade policy; the choice of increasing exports to countries other than the United States was listed third.

15. Refik Erzan and Alexander Yeats, "Free Trade Agreements with the United States: What's in it for Latin America?" World Bank working paper no. WPS 827, Washington, D.C., 1992.

16. John Whalley, "Expanding the North American Free Trade Agreement," Institute for Policy Reform, publication IPR42, Washington, D.C., 1992.

17. For an excellent comparison, see Christopher Stevens, "Western Hemisphere Trade Liberalisation: The Lessons from the European Community Experience," draft of October 1993, used with permission of the author (final article forthcoming, 1994).

18. Jacob Viner, "The Most-Favored-Nation Clause in American Commercial Treaties," *Journal of Political Economy* 32, no. 1 (February 1924): 111.

19. *Inside NAFTA*, February 23, 1994, p. 16. This was not a policy statement but an internal discussion memorandum.

20. There may be a technical as well a substantive problem with Argentina's accession to NAFTA. As envisaged, MERCOSUR would be a customs union with a common external tariff. For the NAFTA countries to obtain free trade in Argentina would require breaching the common tariff. Chile at one point discussed possible accession into MERCOSUR but decided against it in part because Chile's tariff of 11 percent was lower than the projected common external tariff of MERCOSUR. Chile could join only if it raised its import tariffs. Chile has suggested association with MERCOSUR to get around this problem.

21. Stephen Fidler, *Financial Times*, June 7, 1993, p. 21.

22. Stevens, "Western Hemisphere Trade Liberalisation."

23. Peter Morici, *Free Trade in the Americas* (New York: Twentieth Century Fund Press, 1994), 25–32.

Chapter 6

1. Toyota ran an ad in the *Wall Street Journal*, August 3, 1993, p. A13, and undoubtedly in other newspapers as well, under the heading: "We Buy the Best Parts in the World." The gist of the ad is that Toyota now buys more than $4 billion a year of U.S. parts.

2. Max Dupuy and Mark E. Schweitzer, "Are Service-Sector Jobs Inferior?" *Economic Commentary*, Federal Reserve Bank of Cleveland, February 1, 1994.

Bibliography

Augilar Zinser, Adolfo. "Challenges to NAFTA from a Mexican Perspective." *Looking Ahead.* Washington, D.C.: Quarterly opinion publication of National Planning Association 15, no. 2 (July 1993): 23–26.

Berry, Al, Leonard Waverman, and Ann Weston. "Canada and the Enterprise for the Americas Initiative: A Case of Reluctant Regionalism." *Business Economics* 27, no. 2 (April 1992): 31–38.

Bhagwati, Jagdish. *The World Trading System at Risk.* Princeton, N.J.: Princeton University Press, 1991.

Boddez, Thomas M., and Michael J. Trebilcock. *Unfinished Business: Reforming Trade Remedy Laws in North America.* Toronto: C.D. Howe Institute, 1993.

Boltuck, Richard, and Robert E. Litan, eds. *Down in the Dumps: Administration of the Unfair Trade Laws.* Washington, D.C.: Brookings Institution, 1991.

Boske, Leigh B., Robert Harrison, Chandler Stolp, and Sidney Weintraub, directors. *Texas-Mexico Multimodal Transportation.* Policy Research Project Report No. 104. Austin: Lyndon B. Johnson School of Public Affairs, University of Texas, 1993.

Cecchini, Paolo. *The European Challenge 1992: The Benefits of a Single Market.* Hants, England: Wildwood House, 1988.

Cline, William. "'Reciprocity': A New Approach to World Trade Policy?" In *Trade Policy in the 1980s*, edited by Cline, 121–158. Washington, D.C.: Institute for International Economics, 1983.

Coase, R.H. "The Institutional Structure of Production." *American Economic Review* 82, no. 4 (September 1992): 713–719.

Cohen, Isaac. "A New Latin American and Caribbean Nationalism." In *ANNALS of the American Academy of Political and Social Sciences* (issue on "Free Trade in the Western Hemisphere") 526 (March 1993): 36–46.

Commission for the Study of International Migration and Cooperative Economic Development. *Unauthorized Migration: An Economic Development Response.* Washington, D.C.: U.S. Government Printing Office, 1990.

Dupuy, Max, and Mark E. Schweitzer. "Are Service-Sector Jobs Inferior?" *Economic Commentary of Federal Reserve Bank of Cleveland,* February 1, 1994.

Economic Commission for Latin America and the Caribbean. *Open Regionalism in Latin America and the Caribbean.* Document LC/G. 1801 (SES.25/4). Santiago, Chile: United Nations, ECLAC, 1994.

Erzan, Refik, and Alexander Yeats. "Free Trade Agreements with the United States: What's in It for Latin America?" World Bank Working Paper No. WPS 827. Washington, D.C., 1992.

General Agreement on Tariffs and Trade. "Trade Policy Review Mechanism: United States." Document C/RM/S/45, January 19, 1994.

Gore, Al. "Toward a Western Hemisphere Community of Democracies." Address to Mexican, American and Latin American Chambers of Commerce, Mexico City, December 1, 1993.

Hakim, Peter. "President Bush's Southern Strategy: The Enterprise for the Americas Initiative." *Washington Quarterly* 15, no. 2 (Spring 1992): 93–106.

Harris, Richard G. "Trade, Money and Wealth in the Canadian Economy." Toronto: C.D. Howe Institute, Benefactors Lecture, September 14, 1993.

Hart, Michael. *Trade: Why Bother?* Ottawa: Centre for Trade Policy and Law, 1992.

Hufbauer, Gary Clyde, and Jeffrey J. Schott. *NAFTA: An Assessment.* Revised Edition. Washington, D.C.: Institute for International Economics, 1993.

Kantor, Michael, U.S. Trade Representative. Letter to Bill Archer, ranking Republican on Ways and Means Committee, U.S. House of Representatives, as reported in *Inside U.S. Trade,* October 22, 1993.

Katz, Lawrence, chief economist, U.S. Department of Labor. Statement on "Immigration Issues and the North American Free Trade Agreement" before the Subcommittee on International Law, Immigration, and Refugees of the House Judiciary Committee, November 3, 1993.

Kehoe, Timothy J. "Assessing the Economic Impact of North American Free Trade." Discussion Paper No. 265. Center for Economic Research, Department of Economics, University of Minnesota, October 1992.

Kopits, George. "Overview." In George Kopits, *Tax Harmonization in the European Community*, 1–21. Occasional Paper 94. Washington, D.C.: International Monetary Fund, 1992.

Kozolchyk, Boris, ed. *Toward Seamless Borders: Making Free Trade Work in the Americas*. Tucson: National Law Center for Inter-American Free Trade, 1993.

Lipsey, Richard G. "Getting There: The Path to a Western Hemisphere Free Trade Area and Its Structure." In *The Premise and the Promise*, edited by Saborio, 95–116.

Luna, Lucía. "Un Equilibrio Pragmático." *Este País*, no. 27 (June 1993): 2–13.

Martin, Philip L. *Trade and Migration: NAFTA and Agriculture*. Washington, D.C.: Institute for International Economics, 1993.

Mataloni, Jr., Raymond J. "U.S. Multinational Companies: Operations in 1991." *Survey of Current Business* 73, no. 7 (July 1993): 40–58.

Meller, Patricio. "A Latin American Perspective of NAFTA." Santiago, Chile: CIEPLAN (Corporación de Investigaciones Económicas para Latinoamerica). October 1992.

Morici, Peter. *Free Trade in the Americas*. New York: Twentieth Century Fund Press, 1994.

Murphy, Ewell. "Opportunities for U.S. Business in Mexico." *Mexico Trade and Law Reporter* 3, no. 12 (December 1993): 9–15.

Nader, Ralph. "Introduction: Free Trade and the Decline of Democracy." In *The Case against Free Trade: GATT, NAFTA, and the Globalization of Corporate Power*, edited by Nader et al., 1–12. San Francisco: Earth Island Press, and Berkeley, Calif.: North Atlantic Books, 1993.

Naim, Moisés. "Toward Free Trade in the Americas: Building Blocks, Stumbling Blocks and Entry Fees." In *Integrating the Americas: Shaping Future Trade Policy*, edited by Sidney Weintraub. Coral Gables, Florida: University of Miami North South Center, forthcoming 1994.

Nivola, Pietro S. *Regulating Unfair Trade*. Washington: Brookings Institution, 1993.

"PROCAMPO: A New Support Program for the Mexican Farm Sector." Publication distributed by the government of Mexico, 1993.

Robinson, Sherman, Mary Burfisher, Raul Hinojosa-Ojeda, and Karen Thierfelder. "Agricultural Policies and Migration in a U.S.-Mexico Free Trade Area: A Compatible General Equilibrium Analysis." Working Paper No. 617. Department of Agricultural and Resource Economics, University of California at Berkeley, December 1991.

Rosenthal, Gert, Executive Secretary of the Economic Commission for Latin America and the Caribbean. Statement on the occasion of the presidential summit of the Rio Group. Santiago, Chile, October 16, 1993.

Rubio, Luis, and Alain de Remes. *¿Como va a afectar a México el tratado de libre comercio?* México: Fondo de Cultura Económica, 1992.

Runge, C. Ford. *Freer Trade, Protected Environment: Balancing Trade Liberalization and Environmental Interests*. New York: Council on Foreign Relations Press, 1994.

Saborio, Sylvia, ed. *The Premise and the Promise: Free Trade in the Americas*. New Brunswick, N.J.: Transaction Publishers for the Overseas Development Council, 1992.

Scholl, Russell B., Jeffrey H. Lowe, and Sylvia Bargas. "The International Investment Position of the United States in 1992." *Survey of Current Business* 73, no. 6 (June 1993): 42–55.

Stevens, Christopher. "Western Hemisphere Trade Liberalisation: The Lessons from European Community Experience." Draft of October 1993, article forthcoming.

Summers, Robert, and Alan Heston. "The Penn World Table (Mark 5): An Expanded Set of International Comparisons, 1950–1988." *Quarterly Journal of Economics* 106, no. 2 (May 1991): 327–368.

Taylor, Jerry. "NAFTA's Green Accords: Sound and Fury Signifying Little." Cato Institute Policy Analysis Paper No. 198, November 17, 1993.

Thorup, Cathryn L. "Redefining Governance in North America:

Citizen Diplomacy and Cross-Border Coalitions." *Enfoque.* San Diego: Center for U.S.-Mexican Studies, University of California (Spring 1993).

Thorup, Cathryn L. "Redefining Governance in North America: The Impact of Cross-Border Networks and Coalitions on Mexican Immigration into the United States." RAND, DRU 219-FF, March 1993.

United Nations Centre on Transnational Corporations, *World Investment Report 1991: The Triad in Foreign Direct Investment.* New York: United Nations, 1991.

U.S. Council of the Mexico-U.S. Business Committee. "Opportunities for Business Input in NAFTA Procedures and Groups." Paper prepared for internal discussion by Joseph A. Greenwald and Patrick T. Brewer, November 1993.

U.S. Department of Commerce, Bureau of Economic Analysis. *U.S. Direct Investment Abroad: Operations of U.S. Parent Companies and Their Foreign Affiliates.* Washington, D.C.: U.S. Government Printing Office, July 1993.

U.S. Department of Labor, Bureau of Labor Statistics. "International Comparisons of Hourly Compensation Costs for Production Workers in Manufacturing, 1992." Report 844, April 1993.

"U.S. Direct Investment Abroad: Detail for Historical-Cost Position and Balance of Payments Flows, 1992." *Survey of Current Business* 73, no. 7 (July 1993): 88–124.

U.S. Embassy, Mexico City. "Mexico: Economic and Financial Report," Winter 1994.

U.S. Embassy, Mexico City. "Mexico: Foreign Investment Supplement." January 1994.

U.S. International Trade Commission. *Potential Impact on the U.S. Economy and Selected Industries of the North American Free-Trade Agreement.* USITC Publication 2596. Washington, D.C., January 1993.

U.S. International Trade Commission. *Production Sharing: U.S. Imports under Harmonized Tariff Schedule Provisions 9802-00-60 and 9802-00-80, 1989–1992.* USITC publication 2729. Washington, D.C., February 1994.

Viner, Jacob. "The Most-Favored-Nation Clause in American Commercial Treaties." *Journal of Political Economy* 32, no. 1 (February 1924): 101–129.

———. *The Customs Union Issue.* New York: Carnegie Endowment for International Peace, 1950.

Watson, Alexander F. "Toward a Mature Partnership: U.S.-Latin American Relations in the 1990s." Speech by Assistant Secretary of State for Inter-American Affairs before the Institute of the Americas, La Jolla, Calif., March 2, 1994.

Weintraub, Sidney. *The Maquiladora Industry in Mexico: Its Transitional Role.* Working Paper No. 39. Commission for the Study of International Migration and Cooperative Economic Development, June 1990.

_____. *A Marriage of Convenience: Relations between Mexico and the United States.* New York: Oxford University Press, 1990.

_____. "The Rise of North Americanos: A U.S.-Mexico Union." *The Responsive Community* 1, no. 3 (Summer 1991): 64–74.

_____. "Regionalism and the GATT: The North American Initiative." *SAIS Review* 11, no. 1 (Winter–Spring 1991): 45–57.

Whalley, John. "Expanding the North American Free Trade Agreement." Publication 1P R42. Washington, D.C.: Institute for Policy Reform, September 1992.

Wonnacott, Ronald J. *The Economics of Overlapping Free Trade Areas and the Mexican Challenge.* Toronto: C.D. Howe Institute, and Washington, D.C.: National Planning Association, 1991.

Worrell, R. DeLisle. "Economic Integration with Unequal Partner: The Caribbean and North America." Working Paper 205. Woodrow Wilson Center for Scholars, Washington, D.C., 1994.

Yamazawa, Ippei. "Japan's Future Trade and Investment Policies in the Western Hemisphere." In *Integrating the Americas: Shaping Future Trade Policy.* Coral Gables, Florida: University of Miami North South Center, forthcoming 1994.

Zeila, William J. "Merchandise Trade of U.S. Affiliates of Foreign Companies." *Survey of Current Business* 73, no. 10 (October 1993): 52–65.

Index

ISBN 0-275-95118-9

EAN

9 780275 951184

HARDCOVER BAR CODE